LOVE, LAUGH, WOOF

LOVE, LAUGH, WOOF

A Guide to Being Your Dog's Forever Owner

LYNN STACY-SMITH

Archway Publishing books may be ordered through booksellers or by contacting:

Archway Publishing
1663 Liberty Drive
Bloomington, IN 47403
www.archwaypublishing.com
1 (888) 242-5904

Because of the dynamic nature of the Internet, any web addresses or links contained in this book may have changed since publication and may no longer be valid. The views expressed in this work are solely those of the author and do not necessarily reflect the views of the publisher, and the publisher hereby disclaims any responsibility for them.

Any people depicted in stock imagery provided by Thinkstock are models, and such images are being used for illustrative purposes only. Certain stock imagery © Thinkstock.

ISBN: 978-1-4808-3303-6 (sc)
ISBN: 978-1-4808-3304-3 (e)

Library of Congress Control Number: 2016910167

Print information available on the last page.

Archway Publishing rev. date: 08/08/2016

CONTENTS

DEDICATION

This book is dedicated to all of the amazing dogs and humans who have touched my life during the last four decades of dog ownership:

To Snoop, Cinder, Jake, Beau, Dutch and Maggie who are all playing at the Rainbow Bridge together. To Babe for being my very first "soul dog" and my first dog of my own as an adult.

To Destiny for trusting me and helping me find my destiny while I helped her find her forever home.

To Boss for putting up with my affection and puppy snuggles during our visits.

To Jackson and Tinkerbell who fill our home with all of the love, laughter and woofing that it can hold, who fill my heart with joy and who were the inspiration for this book.

To my late mother Karen who was my mom, my best friend, my role model, who not only gave me life but whose literary abilities were passed onto me.

To my late grandmother Fern for being the first published writer in my family tree and putting the housework aside in order to go and enjoy a beautiful day outside.

To my late grandfather Wilson for providing me with resources to make this dream possible.

To my father Bill for always having dogs in our home, for his encouragement, love and support throughout my entire life, for teaching me so much about dogs, for never hesitating to tell me how proud he is.

To my stepmother Donna for being my constant cheerleader, my friend, my confidant and loving parent.

To my stepfather Pete and the lesson that life is short and unpredictable and should be enjoyed.

To my brother Todd and our late brother Scott, for sharing the same love of dogs that I have and for all of our outdoor adventures of our youth.

To my sister-in-law Tanya for being my first sister in my world of all brothers and stepbrothers.

To my best friend Sam and her never ending moral support and love and friendship.

To my business coach Eve for an endless amount of knowledge, moral support and friendship.

To Julie for bringing Jackson and Tinkerbell into the world and for trusting me with their lives.

To Becky for editing my book for me, for being my mom's closest friend, and for helping keep her memory alive.

To Colleen Nedrow of Payton's Photography for her incredible skills and dedication to getting the perfect photo.

To Jake, Paige and Molly for being great kids and our next generation of animal lovers.

And finally to my incredible husband Chuck, my best friend, my rock, my soul mate, my everything, for not freaking out when I quit my corporate job and for his constant love and support. We did not include "becoming a self employed writer for a living" in our marriage vows but he has been loving and supportive through all of the ups and downs of getting this dream off the ground.

EPIGRAPH

"All our dreams can come true, if we have the courage to pursue them." Walt E. Disney

MY LIFE WITH DOGS

During the summer of 1976, the rest of the country was celebrating the 200th anniversary of the signing of the Declaration of Independence when we split from England and became a new country. As a little five year old girl in rural Sparta, New Jersey, though, I was also celebrating the creation of my own new world: a newly blended family.

We had moved from the more urban East Brunswick, New Jersey to the wooded lake country of Sussex County during that summer. My mom had recently remarried and my new dad had legally adopted me. I had two new half-brothers who were my dad's sons from a prior marriage, making us a brand new blended family. We were also in a new house. Mom had left her corporate job and was going back into teaching middle school English, allowing her to be home with me for the first summer in my young life.

We were living in a fairly rural area, and although there were kids my age on our street, I was too painfully shy to try to meet them. I was excited to have two new brothers, but they were only with us every other weekend and half of the summer. Of course Mom was home, and we spent a lot of time together. Even so, she had "adult" things to do around the new house, like unpacking and keeping us fed and in clean clothes, as well as preparing for teaching in the fall.

With a long summer ahead of me, I befriended the one family member who was always willing to play any game that I wanted and never had something more pressing to do. It was that summer that I discovered what it was like to have a Labrador Retriever as my best friend.

Snoop had come into our family with my new dad. She was around two years old when our parents married and was the first dog I had ever had. I had not been around a lot of dogs, but I loved her immediately.

Snoop and I spent countless hours together that summer. She would lie in the grass in our yard with her beautiful head on her paws, just watching while I swung on our swing set. As soon as I was finished swinging, she would follow me to our next game or project, whether it was throwing sticks to her (something I would later get in trouble for after she retrieved a stick instead of a bird on a duck hunting trip with my dad) or just running around the yard. Snoop's presence made everything magical for me that year.

Of course, she was Daddy's dog, and as soon as my dad returned home from work each day, she abandoned me to be by his side, but that seemed normal. After all, she'd spent the whole day with me and I was just grateful for her company. After dinner we would all hang out in the living room and watch TV, Snoop always on the sofa with us, snoozing away and dreaming Labrador dreams.

Later, when we moved to Andover, just one town away from Sparta, I spent another summer without knowing any of the other kids, but that was all right. Snoop and I had hanging out together down to a science by then. My brothers came to stay with us for half the summer, and by then we had developed a sibling bond and we had our own adventures together. Snoop was often along with us on our adventures, since they loved her as much as I did. She was like a fourth sibling to us, even standing in as Chewbacca when we played Star Wars in those magical late 1970s summers.

Snoop was a great dog and had endless patience with us. She let us use her as a pillow, gave us kisses and was a generally amazing friend. Living in the country, we played outside all day every day until our parents made us come inside for the night. Our house was lakefront and Snoop could swim and fetch training dummies right off our own dock all summer. She would chase the hockey pucks of the kids playing ice hockey all winter.

Dad loved to open our back door in the winter when a game of hockey was going on. Snoop would race down the stairs of our deck and then down the long curving path to the lake, run out to the ice, grab the hockey puck and lead the kids around in circles in a game of chase.

"Snoop, give us the puck back," they would shout with laughter filling the air as they all tried to catch her. Eventually she would grow tired of the game, drop the puck, and trot on back up to our house with that fluid Labrador gait and her big pink tongue lolling out of her mouth, ready to resume her spot next to Dad's favorite chair, her adventure complete for the moment.

Over the next eight years, we continued to grow up in that lakefront house on Lake Lenape. We did not realize it then, but it was paradise for kids. We never noticed that we did not have cable TV because we were never inside anyway. We spent all of our time outside, swimming and boating on the lake, riding bikes or playing in the woods where we made up games, built forts and generally had the time of our lives. In 1984, when we did get cable, I watched my first MTV video, Michael Jackson's Thriller, with Snoop lying next to me.

Playing outside subsided somewhat as I became a teenager and I went from shy to social butterfly in literally a weekend. Down came the horse posters and up went the Duran Duran posters. I somehow talked Mom and Dad into getting me my own phone line, and I would lay for hours on my rainbow striped comforter with Snoop next to me as I talked about teenage girl things with my new circle of best friends. Gray hair on her snout, Snoop would lay her head on my butt as I talked and talked. She didn't care how many times I said the word "like" or which boy I liked; she just hung out with me and let me cry on her silky black shoulder when teenage woes got the best of me.

In the fall of 1986, my world was turned upside down by an announcement my dad made to us. By that time my older brother Scott had moved in with us full time. Dad sat us down and said the words, "We are selling the house and moving to Indiana."

I remember sitting at the dinner table open-mouthed, as my world as I knew it shattered to pieces around me. I was fifteen years old and going to move across country to a strange land, leaving all of my friends and my boyfriend behind. I cried into Snoop's neck all night behind the closed door of my bedroom, and refused to speak to anyone.

We moved in December that year. I cried the entire drive across Interstate 80, through Pennsylvania, Ohio, and Indiana, all the way to Valparaiso, a medium sized town in northern Indiana near Chicago.

Moving in December meant that we had a few weeks of school before starting Christmas vacation. My brother and I both met a few friends before break so I had people to eat lunch with and had gone to a few social outings, but I was still facing a boring Christmas break. Fortunately, my brother and I were close and our younger brother Todd would be coming to stay with us for the entire break. Our parents had bought all three of us season passes to the local ski slope as a peace offering. Although it was a fraction of the size ski area that we had enjoyed in New Jersey, we spent most of our vacation skiing. Snoop was still my buddy, but her once black face was now covered in white hair and she preferred snoozing by the fireplace to going on adventures.

One day my parents left us home alone and drove up to Wisconsin. They returned that evening with a new family member: Cinder. Cinder was the sweetest puppy in the litter according to my mom; she had slept peacefully in Mom's lap the entire drive home from the breeder. She had also passed all of Dad's bird dog puppy selection tests with flying colors. Snoop was ready to retire from hunting anyway, and this new puppy arrived at just the right time. We all needed something to get our minds off the fact that we had just moved to an entirely new culture where people used the word "pop" to describe "soda," the ski slope was smaller than the hill in our old back yard, and everyone teased me about my accent.

We would later joke that Cinder had certainly fooled both Mom and Dad by pretending to be docile. As she woke up for the first day in her new world, Cinder began to forge a new reputation for herself: she would be the crazy dog of our family. Our family stories contain plenty of tales of her wacky puppy antics and the things that she destroyed, like the screen door out to the deck or the carpet in front of the sliding door which they were able to stretch a few times until they finally gave up and had to add a bit of extra trim to the side of the floor in that area.

Just like Snoop was attached to Dad, Mom was Cinder's chosen human, a bond that strengthened after Christmas break when we went back to school and Dad back to work. Mom had taken the year off from teaching and was home with Cinder and Snoop every day. When Mom lay on the sofa to read, Cinder curled up in the spot behind her legs. When Mom went outside, Cinder followed.

I was lucky to be Cinder's second favorite human, and the next year when Mom back went to teaching, I loved to come home to be greeted by Snoop and Cinder, their big thick otter tails banging against the hallway in a typical Labrador greeting. I was happy to have two canine best friends, and I certainly needed them as I navigated a new school, made new friends, and got used to life as a Jersey Girl blended with Midwestern teenager.

One spring day during my Junior year of high school, Dad was lying in bed watching TV with Snoop next to him when she started to have terrible seizures, one after another without stopping. He called for my mom and they carried her out to the car in a sheet and raced across town to the meet the vet, whom they had called at home. I was home alone except for Cinder and she laid next to me on my bed for hours while I tried to think about other things but worried about Snoop's prognosis.

When my parents returned that night, I saw my dad in a way that I had never seen him before. Normally he was a strong, successful businessman, a driven Type A personality. His big booming voice and equally big personality were likeable but intimidating at the same time. That night, though, he looked broken as he walked into the house, laid Snoop's collar on the kitchen counter and went up to bed without saying a word.

Mom explained what had happened: the vet could not save our sweet Snoop. We hugged and cried and Cinder licked us nervously, not knowing what had happened to her buddy or why we were both so upset. Snoop had been my first canine love and

I had naively assumed she would always be with us despite the increasingly white muzzle and the extra time that it took her to navigate the stairs.

Cinder was an only dog for a few years, but our house was definitely not quiet with just her in it. My brother Todd had moved in with us by then and with three teenagers in the house, we had frequent guests. Cinder was comfortable with invited guests, but Dad loved to tease my friends by randomly ordering, "Cinder, ATTACK!" when they least expected it, resulting in their screams and our laughter. She was definitely a naughty dog but certainly not an attack dog, although she would growl and slobber whenever the UPS man made a delivery to us.

Cinder was there for every teenage heartbreak that I had, and as a junior and senior in high school, there were plenty of them. Snoop had the easy years; Cinder's silky dog shoulder was wet much more frequently, but she patiently licked my tears away and listened to my stories of teenage heartache.

When it was time for me to leave for college, I did not want to go and Cinder was one of the reasons. I could not remember life without a dog, particularly during stressful and uncertain times, which is how I viewed going away to school. As soon as I arrived at Indiana University, I wanted to return home immediately.

I hated dorm life, hated not having my car, and hated not having my furry best friend. I was rooming with a friend from high school and that made it a little better. Together, we made several friends in our dorm, but that was not enough. I had spent a lifetime living in the country with no immediate neighbors, and Indiana University was like a small city. I went home as often as possible and cried when I had to go back down to school.

I was home for Thanksgiving during my freshman year of college, and one evening, I went to a friend's house to visit. My parents called my friend's house and insisted that I be home at 8 p.m. I was frustrated beyond belief. I was a college freshman! I could not imagine what was up with the insanely early curfew? Children's activities lasted later than that! My dad had been gone all day hunting and Mom and I had spent the entire day together, so I couldn't imagine why I was being summoned home.

As soon as I came into the house, I stomped up the stairs, rounded the corner into the living room and demanded, "What is so important that I had to be home at 8 p.m.? I'm in COLLEGE, for crying out loud" I was standing in the typical indignant eighteen-year-old stance with hands on my hips and one hip jutting out to the side. My parents just stared at me and waited for me to notice the tiny little yellow ball of fur curled up a few feet away.

"OH MY GOD IT'S A PUPPY!" I squealed and threw myself on the ground next to the sleeping puppy as my demeanor instantly changed. He woke up and stretched his adorable puppy stretch. He stumbled over to me with a sleepy puppy gait and I instantly fell head over heels in love with Jake, our new yellow Labrador Retriever.

"Are you still mad at us for making you come home early?" Mom and Dad asked.

I was definitely not.

A few days later I decided that I could not last another semester at Indiana University and my parents and I arranged for me to return home and commute to Indiana University Northwest. I had made the Dean's list at Indiana University, but dorm life was just not for me.

After finals ended, I moved back home, put my things from college away in my room, scheduled my classes at the Indiana University Northwest campus, and started looking for a part time job. Because I was home a week before my mom's Christmas break from her job as a teacher, I was home alone with Jake, who was now a little over three months old and fully in his crazy puppy state.

If you've raised a Labrador puppy, you already know what they are like at three months. The first few days when you bring them home at eight weeks old, they are beautiful little angels, as sweet in nature as they are in appearance. But then they get comfortable and those keen Labrador minds start driving their instinct to explore and learn about their world. Without hands to touch things, they must use their mouth, which translates into long days of removing things from their mouths. I've jokingly referred to this as the "naughty puppy" stage, but in reality they aren't naughty; they are just learning about their environment. However, their way is not the same way we, as humans, would like them to do it since it sometimes involves chewing our stuff. At this stage they rely on us to protect them from chewing and ingesting some of the dangerous things around our homes.

During my week alone with Jake, he explored a variety of things that he quickly found to be a "no" including the glass bulbs from our Christmas tree. We had large old-fashioned lights on our tree back then, made of real glass. My older brother and I were home together the day that Jake bit into the glass bulb. We both sprang into action as soon as we realized what he had done, prying his little puppy jaws apart and cleaning the glass from his mouth. He was squirmy and ready to move on to his next adventure and I was grateful that my brother was there as it was definitely a two-person job. We laid the pieces out on a paper towel to see how much we had collected and were relieved to see that we could recreate the entire bulb.

On a different day, I was alone with Jake and thought that he was sleeping on the floor nearby. All of a sudden I heard a splash and I went running into the room that housed a sunken floor level hot tub and all of Mom's plants. My parents kept a solar cover on it to keep the heat in it.

Jake had stepped off the side of the hot tub onto the solar cover mistaking it for a solid surface. He had fallen in and was caught in the cover, panicking as he splashed around. I ran down the few steps, fully clothed, and snatched him up into my arms.

"Jake, what are you doing? You could have drowned," I cooed to him as I held him to me and headed to grab a towel to dry him.

Of course, Jake was not done with this adventure and he squirmed out of my arms. He landed on the floor and raced through the house at top speed, hitting the kitchen floor and sliding across the 1980s linoleum. He slammed into the refrigerator hard. He sat for a second, shaking off the experience and resumed his Zoomies, a game in which dogs race around at top speed with no destination or purpose other than to run, a crazy soaking wet yellow ball of fur flying through the house at top speed. I saw him heading toward the hot tub room again and I beat him there, closing the French doors before he could do a repeat of his swim.

When Mom arrived home from school a few hours later she asked, "How was Jake? Was he a good boy?"

"Let me tell you about our day," I began, and relayed the story of Jake's adventures to her until we were both howling with laughter.

Jake and our family made it through his puppy years and he grew into an amazing dog. He became a great hunting companion to Dad, and he followed my mom around as she gardened and read during her summer breaks. He was a fun playmate for my brothers and me, especially when we were in the pool. We spent hours in our pool, the five of us all swimming with Jake and

Cinder, throwing balls and their big rubber ducky toy for them to retrieve.

Dad traveled most of the week and Mom's schedule as a teacher meant that she left well before I did each day. She started the habit of bringing the dogs to my room each day as she left for work so they could hang out with me while I slept and then got ready to go to work or school.

"Come on guys, let's go hang out with Lynnie," Mom would say and then she would open my bedroom door. They would scamper into my room and hop up onto the bed with me, both of them knowing the drill; it was time for some more Labrador dreams before we all got up to start the day. I loved those mornings, because it was the only time the dogs could sleep with me and I would fall back asleep with a dog on each side, trapping me under my comforter.

For my junior year of college, my brother and I both went to Purdue University in West Lafayette, and we shared an apartment together. I missed my dogs, but this time I was in the right place and had a great college experience. I had an apartment, my car, freedom, a part time job, and was only an hour and a half away from home if I needed to go and visit Mom, Dad and the dogs.

Senior year, I roomed with one of my best friends from high school and two other girls. We discovered we could volunteer at the local humane society to help walk and socialize with the dogs, which we did often, whenever we needed our doggie fix, usually at least once a week.

After graduating from Purdue University with my Bachelor of Arts in English Literature in 1993, the job market was terrible. I did not have a full time job right away, particularly since I had no idea what I wanted to do with the rest of my young life. I moved back home to my parents' house so I could go on job interviews and save money.

Cinder was starting to slow down a bit and Dad had been asked by a fellow hunter if Jake could be the stud dog to a yellow female Labrador named Molly. He said yes in exchange for the pick of the litter. The puppies were born a few weeks after we moved into a new house that my parents had finished building, and eight weeks later little Beau came home.

Mom and Dad had booked a vacation long before Beau was a glimmer in Jake's mind, so it worked out that I was there to dog sit. Since we had just moved into the house, the fenced in yard was not yet completed. For Cinder and Jake this was not a problem as my father had trained them and their recall was impeccable. I just had to go outside with them and they would come when they were called. As far as little Beau was concerned, Mom told me, "Well, so far it hasn't been an issue, he can't run very fast yet." Yet would be a crucial part of that statement.

Within a day after Mom and Dad headed to their tropical scuba vacation, little Beau did indeed learn to run very fast, with an emphasis on "very." This meant that I also had to run very fast to catch up with him. Fortunately the house was on four acres and there was considerable distance to the road, so I could eventually catch him before he reached that point, but that was a less than idea situation. Jake and Cinder were of no help, watching with tails wagging as I went in pursuit of their little brother. I did not know then that I should have gotten Beau's attention and run the opposite way; that was a lesson I would learn later.

Beau's favorite place to run was under the deck to play in the loose fresh dirt that was under there. Along with the fence not being finished, there was also nothing around the ground floor deck to prevent a young Labrador puppy from running under the deck and digging. I did not mind a digging puppy or even a filthy dirty one from the digging. I did mind a puppy I could not see or control or have a clue as to what he was putting into his mouth while he was under the deck, and it was too low to the ground for me to shimmy under it.

After a few days of this, I outsmarted Beau with the magical invention known as a leash. We didn't have a puppy leash, but I was able to hook the big regular leash through the hooks on his puppy collar. Of course this meant that he could not run around outside to release his puppy energy, but thankfully he had Jake and Cinder to torment while we were inside and they helped to wear him out.

Along with Beau's puppy antics, there was an incident with Cinder and a wasp during the same week. Cinder was notorious for snapping at bugs as they flew past her face. And so on a Sunday in 1994, long before I could hop on the internet to Google a remedy like Benadryl or whisk her off to a 24 hour veterinary clinic, Cinder bit a wasp and was stung inside her mouth. Her head swelled up like a Rottweiler. I sat up with her the entire night to make sure that she was still able to breathe while she panted all night. I had the vet's home phone number and the cordless phone by my side as an emergency precaution.

Cinder, Jake, Beau and I survived Mom and Dad's vacation and I had never been happier to see them arrive at home. I laughed as I relayed the stories about Cinder and the bee and how Beau had in fact found his speed. Laughter had always been a part of how we made it through stressful times; both the big things and the smaller like puppy wrangling without a fence and those stories gradually joined the other funny stories of our family folklore.

Later that summer, I moved into my own apartment across town. I began the habit of going to visit my mom and dad and the dogs several times a week. I still longed for my own dog but

I had also befriended a neighbor with two yellow Labradors who worked long hours and double shifts at his job. I became his dog sitter and was happy to go and let his yellow Labradors out almost every day, spending time playing ball with them, snuggling them and giving them tummy rubs and ear scratches.

When Cinder was around eleven years old, she became sick and passed away. Jake and Beau were still young and loved hunting more than anything else in the world, but they had both begun to have severe grand mal epileptic seizures and Dad was hesitant to take them on bird hunting outings because of their frequent episodes. He had been doing a lot of research on German Shorthaired Pointers and was planning to get one as his next dog. He had located a professional breeder and put a deposit on a puppy from the next litter.

One night when I was visiting for dinner, he told Mom and me, "Now, this puppy is not going to be as warm and loving as the Labs. This breed is a bit more aloof, so don't be hurt if he doesn't want to cuddle and lay on top of you like the Labs."

"That's ok, we've got Jake and Beau to love up on, don't we," I replied in my doggie voice, getting down on the floor to play with them. "Yes, you will give me all the loving I need, right? This new puppy can be all hunting all the time if that's what he wants!"

A few months later Dutch came home and I headed over to my parents' house to meet the "aloof" puppy. As soon as I walked in the house I spotted him curled up in a ball within the rungs of the kitchen chair, a silky dark brown covered with white speckles and large round brown patches. He woke up a few minutes after I arrived and we took him outside to relieve himself.

His business finished, I could not resist scooping him up. He was one of the most beautiful puppies I had ever seen in my life, and how aloof could a puppy possibly be?

Dutch nested into my arms and started to lick my face. "Oh yes, you are so aloof, you don't want anything to do with us humans, do you?" I cooed to him in my singsong puppy voice.

"Well, don't expect that to last long; he's going to be all about the birds," Dad said.

Dutch did indeed grow up to be a fantastic bird dog, but when he was not training or hunting with my father, he was one of the most goofy and funny dogs I have ever known. He also failed brilliantly at being aloof and was one of the most snuggly dogs to be a part of our family.

Mom and Dad's dogs, Jake and Beau, were like brothers to me and I had lived with both of them before moving out on my own. When Dutch was a few months old, I was called upon to dog-sit for my parents while they went on another scuba trip and I was more than happy to spend time with the dogs and a swimming pool instead of my 20-something apartment that had neither dogs nor a pool. It was during this trip that I truly fell in love with Dutch as the third of my dog brothers.

I had not realized that a breed could have any more energy than a Labrador Retriever until I spent a few weeks with a young German Shorthaired Pointer. Dutch's energy was endless and his antics were hilarious. His legs seemed to grow before the rest of him and his paws were too big for the rest of his body for quite a long time. He loved doing Zoomies regardless of whether or not Jake or Beau joined him, and I would just laugh as he zipped by me, a big gangly brown and white ball of energy.

Beau was the best helper with Dutch that I could ever imagine. When Dutch would start to get into trouble and play with something he should not, Beau was right there to distract him, literally putting bones and toys into Dutch's mouth or engaging him in a game to distract him from whatever contraband item that he was about to explore. From the first week that they were together, Dutch and Beau were inseparable, whether sleeping or awake. One afternoon I caught them sleeping on the fireplace hearth together, with both of them on their sides, legs sticking straight out, and Dutch perfectly nestled up against Beau like a set of Russian nesting dolls.

Dutch's favorite habit was to carry something in his mouth at all times, particularly when someone came to the front door. Usually there was a toy nearby that he could grab, with his favorite being his stuffed hedgehog toy that my mom had nicknamed Hedgy. If there was no toy nearby, he would grab a pillow or the towel that Mom kept by the back door to wipe muddy paws. One time he dragged the entire king sized comforter off my parent's bed all the way down the stairs to the front door when a friend of mine stopped by to visit while I was dog sitting.

With three dogs now at my parents' house, I visited even more often, particularly in the summer, since Mom was a teacher and did not work during the summer. Of course, I loved my parents but I was starting to feel lost without a dog in my own home. I jumped at every chance to dog sit for them, and hated to go home to a dogless existence. With the exception of college, I had never lived without a dog, and I desperately craved having a dog of my own.

It was a few years later when I was 27, my dad called me and mentioned a dog who would forever change my life. "It's too bad you can't have a dog," he said, "My friend has a beautiful black Labrador who is staying at his hunting preserve, and he's trying to find a home for her. She's gun-shy and won't hunt, but she'd make a great pet for you."

My landlord had told me that dogs were not allowed, but because he was a private homeowner instead of a large company,

I decided on a whim to plead my case, giving him my background with dogs and my plan for exercising the dog and keeping her from destroying the apartment. To my surprise he agreed, and I arranged to go meet the dog.

I went with Dad to meet her on Thanksgiving morning. She was a two-year-old female Labrador Retriever whose owners were elderly and had both fallen into poor health. They could no longer care for a young, rambunctious dog. They lived near my dad's friend's bird hunting preserve and had asked him to re-home her for them, knowing that he was a great resource for people who would properly love and care for a big Labrador Retriever.

We pulled up and Dad went off in search of his friend. I walked toward the fenced in backyard where I could see the dog. She came running as I let myself in through the gate and I smiled as I watched her wiggle-run her way to me. She had classic Labrador beauty and personality and I bent down to pet her. I looked at the tag on her collar and said her name out loud, "Babe." Her ears went up and her tail started wagging more furiously. "Hi, Babe," I said again, and she wiggled even harder.

Dad called to me and as I turned, I took a step backwards and suddenly lost my balance. I fell to the ground hard and I was confused as I looked around to see what had happened, but within seconds of landing on the ground I had a mass of wriggling black fur on top of me. It was Babe, her tail still wagging furiously and her tongue licking my entire face. I had stepped into a huge hole that she had dug in the dirt, which I would later tease her by telling her she had done that on purpose so she could make me "fall" in love with her.

After we left, I started to obsess over whether or not I should adopt her. I had fallen in love with her, but I had also grown up learning from my parents that this was as serious as if I was bringing another human into the world. Could I afford her vet bills? Could I afford her food? What if I had to move for some reason? Could I find another place that would allow me to have a large dog? I was back and forth on my decision multiple times an hour. Yes, I would take her. No, I should not. Yes, I would. No, I should not.

Finally I decided to go and get my girl. Babe was two when I adopted her and was an incredible dog. She was fully trained, super sweet and snuggly and was at the perfect age for a Labrador; she had boundless energy but great manners and I instantly knew she was meant to be mine.

Over the next decade, Babe would go almost everywhere with me, on walks through downtown Valparaiso and hikes at the Indiana Dunes and the local parks. Not having a fenced yard meant that we walked multiple times a day. She loved to stalk squirrels and sniff the new smells as we varied our routes, but for her the best part was meeting new people on our walks. At least once a week, we walked through the nature trails at different parks on longer hikes and sometimes we went to the circular walking track in the middle of town, which she particularly loved because of all of the other walkers and joggers who frequented the track.

Babe also accompanied me to my parents' homes on a regular basis. Right before I adopted Babe, my parents had divorced and the three dogs stayed with Mom because the three of them were too bonded to each other to be separated.

Babe particularly enjoyed playing with Dutch, engaging in long games of chase and Bitey-Face. Sometimes, she and Beau played, and I loved to watch them all race around the yard together. Jake joined in every now and then, but as the elder statesman of the group, he was mostly interested in snoozing in the sunshine or checking out the perimeter of the yard.

Babe and I also stayed at the house whenever Mom went on vacation or out of town for the night. Having all four dogs with me was one of my favorite things. I felt like their pack leader whenever we went outside together as they trotted along happily beside me or settled in for the evening, all of us sharing the sofa and blankets. At night when I watched the dogs for Mom, I would sleep in her King-sized bed with the four dogs all around me. I think that Babe was just as happy as I was to be part of the pack; she was so good-natured and flexible that she just settled in with the rest of the dogs whenever we were there.

Once a week we usually ended up visiting my dad and my stepmother, too. After awhile, Dad brought home a young German Shorthaired Pointer puppy whom they named Boss, and Babe would play with him, too. Boss was young and crazy and Babe learned where the edge of his invisible fence was and would stand just on the outside of it whenever he became too much puppy for her to handle.

Babe also came with me when I ran errands, to friends' homes and outdoor parties. For much of Babe's life I worked as a waitress and she and I would walk to the bank every few days and make deposits of my tips at the walk-up window. It was the only bank branch with a walk-up window, and the tellers always had biscuits waiting for Babe. She knew she would get biscuits and would jump up and put her paws on the shelf outside the window in anticipation, a move that was incredibly adorable and always earned her an extra treat. On rainy days, we would drive and she would thrust her snout into the bank drive-up tube to get her treat. Every once in awhile a teller would forget a treat and she would cock her head and look at me in that cute tilted-head Labrador way, and I would give her double the treats when we got home.

In April 2005, when Babe was around 11, we moved to Illinois after I ended a long relationship and needed a fresh start and a shorter commute to work. I had been commuting from Indiana to Illinois for a year, a drive that took up far too much time and gas and required me to arrange a midday potty break for Babe every day of the week.

After all of my boxes and furniture were in my new place, I locked the apartment door behind the movers and it was just Babe and me. I became more and more lonely and freaked out as thought about how far away I had moved from my friends and my mom, the same mom who had always lived in at least the same town as me except for when I was away at college, the mom who was battling Stage 4 Breast Cancer but who worried so much about my long commute that she had encouraged me to move to ease her mind about me doing such a horrible commute. I sat down on my sofa, surrounded by boxes, and cried.

As I cried, Babe came to comfort me and laid her head on my leg. My tears flowed down and made a wet spot on her beautiful head. I hugged her to me and gave myself a pep talk and pulled myself together. And then I dug out her bowl and food, fed her supper, ordered a pizza and we settled in to our new home, just the two of us.

The next day I woke in my new home and declared to her that the boxes could wait, that we were going to set out to find a new favorite park in our new town, and so Babe and I set out on a new adventure. She had not understood a word that I had said but she followed along happily, her big otter tail wagging like normal.

In December, I got the call from my stepfather that my mom had been taken to the hospital via ambulance and that I should come to Indiana. I grabbed some clothes for several days, put Babe in the car, and headed to Indiana to see my mom in the hospital. I dropped Babe off at her house to hang out with Beau and Dutch. Jake had passed away a few years previously. I wasn't sure how long I would be in Indiana but I never went anywhere without Babe, especially since I had not yet found good dog sitters in Illinois.

Mom died that week, on Christmas Day, 2005. That night as I slept on the sofa in my mom and stepfather's living room, I cried steadily throughout the night with the three dogs to comfort me. It was caring for the dogs and making the funeral arrangements with my stepfather that kept me going through each day.

When Mom died, Beau was a senior dog who had lived a life battling epilepsy. He had led a great life, but his grand mal seizures sometimes lasted hours, as he would go in and out of a seizure. Our family veterinarian had been amazed that Beau lived through each episode, but live through them he did. Beau could go through an hour-long seizure and hop up and grab his tennis ball as if nothing had happened. He took several medications and had recently gone on Potassium Bromide, which had caused him to gain a substantial amount of weight.

Before Potassium Bromide, Beau had been a normal sized male Labrador of about 80 pounds. After going on the drug he was over 120 pounds and the weight combined with his age were wreaking havoc on his ability to walk. I could tell that he was in pain and it broke my heart to watch him walk down one small step and fall to the ground just to go outside for a potty break. He struggled to get up and down although once he was up he seemed to be his happy Beau self.

The last day that Mom was awake she had said to me, "I think Beau is going to follow me, isn't he?" and I said that yes, I would probably take him to the vet soon because he was having such a hard time getting around. "That's ok, he's ready," she said, nodding in agreement. I knew that she had been ready, too. I promised her that I would take care of Dutch and that he would come and live with Babe and me in Illinois for the rest of his life.

One week after Mom passed away I took Beau to the vet, my heart breaking as I drove him there. I lay on the floor spooning him like he had once spooned Dutch while the vet administered the shots. I stroked his side and told him how much I loved him and that I hoped that he would meet Mom in heaven, that the Rainbow Bridge that people talked about was real and that a healthy Mom would throw tennis balls in heaven to a healthy and young Beau for all of eternity, and that Jake and Cinder would be there too, and Snoop whom he had never met. I prayed that Mom and her pack of beloved Labradors would be in heaven, united again forever.

With Dutch in the back seat of my car I drove to Illinois scared to death of what I was doing. The apartment that I rented had a dog policy that allowed one or two dogs with a maximum weight of 60 pounds. Babe weighed 80, and Dutch was 90. I was terrified that we would be evicted without a place to live and no family in the vicinity. My closest family members were in Florida, too far away to crash on the sofa with two dogs without quitting my job, although I would have used that backup plan if I absolutely had to before I gave up Dutch or Babe.

Transitioning Dutch to a life in an apartment complex with just leashed walks to wear him out was difficult. He was ten years old but a ten-year-old German Shorthaired Pointer has more energy than some breeds do as puppies, and Dutch was a typical energetic GSP. Dutch had not been leashed walked in months because of Mom's cancer and the convenience of her fenced in yard. He was used to living in a single-family home instead of a busy apartment complex, and he barked at every noise. Confused and desperate for my attention, he shoved Babe out of the way whenever I tried to pet her, pushed her aside to inhale her food, yanked my arm out of the socket on walks, broke two leashes and generally had me in tears for weeks on end, probably acerbated by my grief over losing my mother.

Eventually, though, with lots and lots of patience, we made it through the rough times and I found myself happy to have sweet Dutch with me, to the point where I started to think that if Mom could magically come back, I wouldn't want to give him back to her. Getting from extreme frustration to our happy existence was one of the biggest challenges I had ever had as a dog owner.

I learned that the maintenance man had a soft spot for German Shorthaired Pointers, and he assured me that I was not going to be turned in to the apartment management for having 2 large dogs, which took a ninety-pound weight off my shoulders. I got Dutch to walk nicely on the leash again. I mastered the art of walking both of them at once and he joined our journeys to the local parks and trails. We became a trio, Babe, Dutch and me, and I felt blessed to have two special furry babies to keep me company. I looked forward to taking them on hiking adventures each weekend and to snuggling up with them in front of the TV or with a book each evening.

I met my future husband in December 2006 and in April 2007, Babe, Dutch and I moved into his house that he shared with his three children and their eight year old rescued Basset Hound, Maggie. Three kids and three dogs! We, as adults, were clearly outnumbered, and we couldn't have been happier about it.

Maggie, the Basset Hound, loved Babe immediately and followed her everywhere, snuggling up against her while they napped. It took her longer to enjoy Dutch's company, but after a few weeks our three dogs were living in harmony. Life with a senior Labrador Retriever, an almost senior German Shorthaired Pointer, and a Basset Hound meant a lot of very different dog personalities, and our trio gave us plenty to laugh about. We loved how Maggie would walk right under the other two instead of walking around them, and our hearts melted each time we saw different variations of the dogs sharing the same bed. Babe and Dutch loved the kids instantly and vice versa, and I was happy that they no longer had to wait for me for nine hour days while I was at work.

At the start of the following summer in June 2008, Maggie started having accidents in the house and in her crate that did not make sense. She also started moving slowly and seemed to have no energy. We took her to the vet wondering if she had Lyme disease, as we had recently found a tick on her ear and some of the symptoms matched those of Lyme disease.

We were way off of our self-diagnosis. Maggie did not have a disease or virus, she had developed Intervertebral Disc Disease, and it was rapidly growing worse. In the few days she spent at the vet's office for testing and observation she became unable to hold her bladder or walk; she was paralyzed from the middle of her back down to her back paws. Without surgery, we would have no other choice than to put her to sleep.

Surgical quotes for canine neurosurgeons were coming in to us at the cost of around $15,000. There was no way we could afford that, and all five of our hearts broke as we searched for alternatives. After we had exhausted all of our options we decided to bring her home for one more night and to put her to sleep the following day. The thought of life without our Maggie was unbearable and the kids and I were inconsolable. My husband stayed strong for all of us, but I know that his heart was breaking for this sweet dog that he had rescued from an abusive past.

By a miracle, though, we found a place at the very last second to do her surgery. My Alma mater, Purdue University, known for their veterinary program, would do the surgery and their initial quote was $2000. We jumped at the opportunity and my husband made a makeshift bed on the front seat of his minivan for Maggie, and off they went to Purdue. The kids and I stood watching in the front yard as they pulled away, all of us with tears in our eyes and prayers in our hearts that Maggie would come back to us.

Maggie sailed through surgery and within days had control of her bladder again. She spent two weeks at Purdue under their watchful eye before coming home to us for several months of kennel rest and physical therapy. The Purdue veterinary team showed my husband how to do the physical therapy exercises, and he and Maggie hit the road back to Illinois.

Even a few days of kennel rest are tough on a dog, yet Maggie had several months ahead of her. She seemed to intuitively know that it was where she needed to be, as did Babe and Dutch, who laid near her kennel to keep her company and watched from a few feet away as we performed PT with her four times a day. We had a special sling to use to take her outside so that she could propel herself with her front legs and we could carry her back end for her with the sling. We took all of our potty breaks outside that way throughout the day, a leash in one hand and the sling in the other, holding her back legs above the ground as we walked and then setting her feet down on the ground so that she could eliminate her bowels and bladder.

Maggie was an amazing little patient and as the weeks went by we could feel her muscles coming back. She started pushing back on our hands during therapy and one magical day, we set her hind end on the ground and she stood on her own, wobbly but standing. A month later she took her first steps on her own and three months after surgery she was cantering around the yard chasing rabbits. She had a funny little gait and ran somewhat like a bunny herself, but our Maggie was back in action.

In July 2009 my husband and I got married. Four months later in October 2009, I came home from work to find Babe in a scene straight out of the book The Art of Racing in the Rain. She was splayed out in the kitchen, slipping and sliding and unable to stand up in a pool of urine and diarrhea, a terrified expression on her face. My husband was also working that day and I had no idea how she had been like that. She was thirteen years old and her back legs were getting worse by the day, and she had terrible diarrhea accidents on our carpet at least once a week overnight because she could not climb the stairs to reach us to wake us. I solved that issue by setting an alarm in the middle of the night to give her an additional potty break or sometimes sleeping on the sofa so that she could wake me up to take her outside, but no matter what I did, I could not make her legs stronger.

The next month, I came home from work one night and she could hardly walk. She kept falling backward and sitting at an awkward angle, still trying to follow me from room to room. Every time she stopped, she wobbled from side to side. Sometimes she would fall backwards back into a sitting position and was unable to stand back up.

She followed me as I removed my coat, shoes and put my purse on the dining room table. As I turned around to pet her she fell back once more, her legs splayed at an awkward angle, completely unable to get up and a sad and hopeless look on her face. I knelt on the floor next to her to try to help her up and she fell back again. We did it a few more times before I sat on the floor and had her lie down next to me. I called the vet from that spot on the floor as if on some sort of autopilot and scheduled an appointment the next day to put my sweet Babe to sleep.

That night I felt like I was in a terrible nightmare. I slept downstairs with her, lying on her dog bed next to her. The time ticked away and I desperately longed to cancel the appointment, but I knew it was time. The next morning, once again I lay on the floor of a veterinarian's office, this time lying with my face close to hers, like we had always lain. I stayed there next to my best friend, stroking her face until the vet said the words, "That's it, she has passed."

Only then did I begin to wail with grief. I did not care where I was or that I was in public. I had already signed all of the paperwork and I headed to the waiting room where my husband waited for me. I went straight to the car where I cried as hard as I had cried when my mom died, nearly howling with the pain. I wanted her back immediately, I regretted the decision, and my husband held me and gently reminded me of how much pain Babe had been in, how much a dog needed to be able to walk and get around to have a good quality of life, and that I had the done the right thing, the humane thing for my girl.

Losing Babe was as surreal as losing my mom. It felt like a part of me was gone and would never return. A few days later, I forced myself back to the land of the living and threw myself into caring for Dutch and Maggie. I did not know then that in just another fourteen months, I would be doing the same thing yet again with Dutch, after cancer in his spleen took over his entire body.

After Dutch died I did not want to get out of bed. They had all been lost too close together: Mom, Beau, Babe and Dutch, one after another. They had been my lifelines before I met my husband and stepchildren and now they were all gone.

Dutch died the day of a massive blizzard and after we arrived home from the veterinarian's office without him I wrapped myself up in his blanket and went to bed and cried for the entire next day. I emerged after my husband went to work so that I could care for Maggie, and she snuggled up next to me and we mourned our sweet Dutchdog while it snowed inch after inch after inch. The kids were at their mother's house and it was just the two of us for twenty-four hours. Maggie loved to snuggle and be held and I clung to her, both of us wrapped in Dutch's blanket. She licked my face as I cried and I thought about how my husband may have rescued her, but she was the one rescuing me at that moment.

The next day I started looking at German Shorthaired Pointer rescues. My husband saw the dogs I was looking at, senior GSPs in need of loving homes and he nodded along kindly with each one that I pointed out. They all looked like Dutch, the dark liver with white ticking. But none of them were Dutch.

"I think you're trying to replace Dutch," he very gently said to me one night, "and I know how much you love your Labradors and how you've talked about how you've never been without one and that you wanted to get another." I listened and watched as he told me that he'd received a recommendation from a friend of a friend and pulled up the website of a professional/hobby breeder. Tears streamed down my face again as I scrolled through her pages of males, females, puppies and read about her philosophy on breeding dogs.

"Yes, I want another Labrador; you are right. And I want a black male and I want to name him Jackson and I'll call him Jax. Do you remember I said that was the perfect dog name?" I said with my first smile in weeks.

JACKSON AND TINKERBELL

We're Going to Jackson was born on March 8, 2011. He was one of four roly-poly black male Labradors in his litter. Our breeder sent us the photos of the litter every week starting the day they were born, and I fell in love with all of them instantly. I was not sure which one would become ours, but it did not matter. I would love whichever one was destined to become Jackson.

When Jax was just two and a half weeks old our breeder checked on the pups and their mother one last time before settling in to watch a bit of TV and then going to bed. The whelping pen was just off of her living room and suddenly she heard one of the puppies shrieking in pain. She ran in to find little Aqua, his temporary name as identified by the piece of aqua colored yarn on his neck, squealing in pain and laying up near his mother's elbow while nursing.

A trip to the vet revealed that his back leg had been broken, most likely from his mother rolling over and accidentally trapping the leg under her elbow. Fortunately it was a clean break of a smaller bone that was somewhat protected by a bigger bone and would likely heal without a cast, but neither the vet nor our breeder had worked with a broken leg in a puppy so young and could not be sure what the future held for him.

Because we were the fourth set of puppy buyers to choose our pup, our breeder emailed us to let us know that it might come down to the puppy with the broken leg being the only puppy left. She understood if we did not want to take him because of his leg but she felt that we should consider him because it was a clean break and her vet did not expect it to cause him any issues later in life or impact his growth. Over the next few weeks we would email frequently with stories of his progress and what an incredible little puppy he was in the way that he dealt with his injury.

A few weeks before the puppies were ready to go home, I emailed our breeder and asked, "I know there's a specific order to how people pick puppies, but is it possible for us to request Aqua puppy, the one with the broken leg? We want him; we don't want to just wait to see if he's left last. We feel like he is supposed to be our special boy."

She wrote back that she was thrilled that we had made that decision and that yes, she would reserve little Aqua for us. When he was eight weeks old we would drive to her farm in Iowa to pick up our special little puppy, our Aqua Dog who we would name Jackson, the puppy who would lick away all of the tears I had cried for Babe and Dutch.

On May 4, 2011, my husband and I arrived in the small town in Iowa where our breeder lived and checked into a hotel. We had dinner and ran to Wal-Mart after realizing that we did not have a travel crate and that picking up a new puppy without a travel crate was like going to the hospital to have a baby without a car seat installed and ready. We had a wire kennel waiting for him at home, the equivalent of a bassinet or crib; we had just forgotten the travel part. We set up the new crate in the minivan along with the blankets we had brought for him and headed back to the hotel. Maggie was home with the dog sitter, her last night as an only dog.

I was full of nervous energy and could not sleep even though I knew it was the last full night of sleep that I would have for several weeks because of the puppy potty breaks that would be necessary all night. We watched TV in our hotel room and each minute ticked by. I fell asleep at some point but woke early. Reminding myself that sleep as I knew it was about to end, I tried to fall back asleep but my body was humming with excitement so I showered and got ready to go meet our puppy.

Finally we headed out to our breeder's home, over hilly country roads and through fields that were plowed and planted for spring. We turned down a dirt road, pulled into the gravel driveway, and parked next to the house. At the front of the driveway was our breeder's boarding kennel and we were greeted by several barking dogs that were enjoying the beautiful day outdoors in their kennel runs.

Meeting our breeder felt like a blind date. What if she didn't like us in person? What if she didn't like the look of us or think that we were serious enough Labrador owners? I couldn't handle the heartache of not picking up the puppy who it seemed was fated to be ours, especially after ten weeks of waiting to meet him and hold him.

We knocked on the door and our breeder welcomed us into her home. Six or seven beautiful Labrador retrievers in black and yellow ran to greet us, all perfectly polite with their tails wagging their entire bodies. We were sniffed and greeted and I felt like I was in my version of heaven as I bent down to pet them. In typical Labrador fashion, they weaved in and out between us, all vying for their chance to greet the strangers who had certainly come to see them.

I had tears streaming down my face from joy; I had forgotten how much I loved this breed in the year and a half that Babe had been gone. These dogs made me realize how much I had missed her. I knew we had made the right decision to add another Labrador to our family. I also knew that we had chosen the exact right place to get him.

After the Labrador greeting, we were excited to finally meet our breeder, who I had gotten to know via email but was meeting for the first time in person. While I introduced my husband, I noticed that the Labradors had, on their own, all gone back to their dog beds throughout the house, perfectly behaved and ready to resume their playing, napping or toy chewing. There were a few crates with open doors and one of the dogs made himself comfortable in it. The house was clean and neat and somehow did not smell one bit of dog despite there being so many.

"So do you want to finally meet your puppy?" she asked, and I remembered why we were there in the first place. I was so happy just from the warm welcome that I had received from the other dogs that I momentarily forgotten why we were there.

She opened the door to a small crate to let him out and told us that he was in there to keep him from being stepped on by the bigger dogs when we arrived. As little Aqua Puppy met us for the first time, I had hot tears of joy streaming down my face again. I picked him up and held him to me and he licked my face, wiping away the tears as fast as they came. His little tail wagged furiously and I buried my face in his soft puppy coat.

"Hi, Jackson," I said, "You're going to be my dog. I love you already and we are going to give you the best life possible, I promise you."

We went over all of the paperwork, including the AKC registration, his microchip, and her policy of not abandoning him in a shelter: she would take him back at any time in his life if we needed her to. She gave a brief overview of the training information that she was sending with us, basic food and health maintenance tips, and all of the information that a puppy owner would need. Of course we were experienced dog owners but I was happy to get any and all information, particularly because we had spent so many years caring for senior dogs that to have a puppy in the house was suddenly like having a newborn after sending your last human child away to college.

We headed off to the car with Jackson, along with a 27-pound bag of dog food, a huge beef knuckle bone for him to occupy himself on the 6-hour ride home, and our folder of paperwork and educational materials.

"Can I take a moment with him?" our breeder asked.

"Of course!" I replied.

I could see tears in her eyes as I heard her say to him, "Now, we talked about this, every dog grows up and gets a job." She snuggled him one last time before sending him with us.

"Thanks," she said, after handing him back to me, "I spent so much extra time with him, caring for that leg."

I replied, "Thank you so much for doing what you do, for raising these beautiful Labradors and loving them so much."

After some more goodbyes, we put Jackson into his travel crate and started our six-hour journey back to Illinois. My husband was driving, I was in the passenger side, and Jackson was in his crate. We had positioned the crate so its door was within our reach and Jackson could see us in case he was scared. I expected some whimpering or crying as he dealt with the newness of the situation, but instead he settled down to the task of chewing his beef knuckle and quietly gnawed away for the first hour.

After awhile, when he was tired from chewing his bone, he pawed the blanket into a small pile as a pillow and curled up and went to sleep. I checked on him every ten minutes for the first two hours, twisting in my seat to make sure that he was ok so often that my neck started to get sore. "He's fine, he's sleeping," my husband told me gently.

Halfway through the journey, we stopped at a rest area for a potty break for our pup. Not used to walking on a leash or wearing a collar yet, he was more obsessed with trying to bite the leash than with walking to the grass, so I picked him up to take him to a grassy area.

As I carried him, a yellow jacket buzzed around our heads and I covered his little face with my hand to protect him from the bee, despite a long time bee phobia. I suddenly felt a sharp stinging sensation in my neck and realized that the bee had stung me. "Ouch!" I exclaimed and my husband turned around quickly, "I just got stung by a bee on the neck!" I exclaimed, as I moved my hand from protecting Jackson, "I'm just glad it got me and not him," I said, realizing that I already had a mother's love for this tiny puppy who had only been mine for two hours.

Once Jackson had emptied his bowels and bladder we headed back to the minivan, gave him some water, and started the rest of our journey home. Back in his crate, he gave a few little whimpers but quickly opted for chewing his bone instead, and then he drifted off to sleep again just like he had the first time.

We arrived home around dinnertime and prepared to introduce Maggie to the new puppy. Having read some articles on how to introduce a new puppy to the an adult dog, we chose to do the introduction in the grassy area in the middle of our cul-de-sac, a neutral area that was not Maggie's own territory.

I stayed outside with Jackson, and my husband went to get Maggie. She was ecstatic to see me when he brought her into the cul-de-sac until she saw little Jackson. We had expected a happy meet and greet since he was so little and helpless, but what we had was an angry, snarling Basset Hound who seemed determined to show him that she did not in fact welcome his presence. Each time we let them approach each other she growled and lunged at him. Although he did not seem terribly upset, we were afraid that she would hurt him.

I was stunned by Maggie's response; she had accepted Babe and Dutch immediately and they were older than her, all grown dogs when they met. Of course she had been a younger dog then also, but I was still shocked that she would welcome two grown dogs into her home but not a tiny puppy.

Fortunately, Jackson still required two more weeks of kennel rest and limited activity to let his leg heal, plus he was completely worn out from the journey and all of the new things that he had experienced that day. We gave him water and his dinner and put him in the large wire crate that we had set up in our living room for him, along with his first toy, a plush mallard duck that I had purchased just for him. He immediately lay down with the duck as a pillow. Although we could see him fighting sleep, he was sound asleep within minutes.

The next day we took Jackson for his first veterinary appointment at our own vet. He charmed the staff, got his microchip and shots like a champ, and we received some great advice on how to encourage Maggie to stop wanting to rip him to pieces and to perhaps even like him.

When we returned home, I stayed outside with Jackson once again and my husband went inside to get Maggie. Our veterinarian had advised us to take them on walks together to make sure that Maggie associated something fun like a walk with her new baby brother. Maggie loved leash walks so we decided to try that idea immediately.

Maggie and my husband went first, with Jackson and me following along behind them at a distance. This also helped make Jackson forget about the leash that was so foreign to him after spending his first eight weeks of his life on a farm. He trotted along happily, not sure whether he wanted to sniff each and every spot of ground or focus on keeping up with Maggie. His interest in Maggie was winning, though, and he scampered along behind her so that we caught up halfway through out walk.

After awhile, Jackson and I started to walk side by side with Maggie and my husband and we were thrilled that although Maggie kept checking him out, she did not snarl or growl. We ran into our neighbors who were as happy to see her as they were to see the new puppy, rubbing her ears and telling her, "We usually only get to see you from a distance," because our back yards faced each other but were separated by a few other houses and their fenced in yards.

After about 15 minutes of walking, we headed home and let Maggie check out the puppy up close. This time, there was no growling or snarling, and she even let him drink out of the water bowl with her. We were elated with the progress we had made.

After so many big experiences, his first vet appointment, puppy vaccinations and a walk around the block, Jackson was worn out and we put him in his kennel. Within minutes he was sound asleep and Maggie laid near the kennel watching him before falling asleep herself, just a few feet away.

Each day Maggie grew to like her new brother a little more, and we grew one day closer to his leg being completely healed. Then Jackson would be allowed to roughhouse and play. Now we were able to take walks, but he could not run and jump, which is all a young puppy wants to do. He was beyond good at being in his crate, and we made sure he had plenty of chew toys, bones, Kongs and other things to occupy his mind. I felt overwhelmed with guilt at how much time he had to spent in the crate and kept reminding myself that it was the vet's orders and for the good of his entire future as a dog. We snuggled with him on our laps and Maggie started to sleep near his crate as a habit.

Finally we reached the two-week mark and headed off to the vet's office for a new x-ray of his little broken leg. He was so good with the veterinary staff and so accustomed to being handled that he just laid there for them to X-ray him, no sedation needed to get perfect photos.

Within minutes we were ushered into the vet's office while the technicians and assistants ooh-d and ahh-d over our adorable little puppy and our vet pulled up the new X-rays on the computer as well as the ones that our breeder's vet in Iowa had emailed to him.

The verdict: his leg had healed beautifully and completely and he was given the all clear to lead a normal puppy life. Just as our breeder had explained, the break was as ideal as a break could be, nice and clean, so it had healed beautifully. Just as she and her vet predicted, our vet agreed that this break would probably never bother him again later in life.

Once at home, our little black ball of fur was able to run and play, and he did. He was ready, particularly the last week of kennel rest. His energy and confidence had been building steadily and he raced around the yard at top speed, his first lap of puppy Zoomies. We let Maggie out and she barked and barked as he raced around her in circles but eventually we realized that it was her version of playing.

We spent the summer of 2011 raising Jackson, training him in obedience, and teaching him the rules of the house. We watched him play with Maggie, at first worried that she would injure him and his formerly broken leg, and then worrying about him injuring her as he grew bigger and stronger and quickly surpassed her in height.

We watched awestruck as Jax figured out a way to play with Maggie, working around her physical disabilities as if he knew that she couldn't do the same things that he could. He played tug with her, a game normally forbidden because of the pressure it put on her back, but only pulled back a little. He played Bitey-Face, a classic dog game in which they pretend to bite each other but do not actually make contact with each other, with her but never jumped on her, never mounted her, never rolled her around or slammed into her. They played Zoomies together; their version involved Maggie standing in one spot barking while Jax took care of all of the Zoomies. "He's a special dog," echoed in our heads as we watched them become best friends, both of them once broken but now healed, our mismatched bonded pair.

Jax was a quick study on house training and gave no complaints about going into his kennel when we had to leave. He learned his obedience commands very quickly at puppy classes, and was overall an amazing dog, so chilled and relaxed with every new experience. We had received a checklist of things at our puppy class that he should be exposed to at a young age, and we went through it item by item, using it as a literal checklist.

Bicycles, check.
Loud motorcycle, check.
Kids on skateboards, check.
Fireworks, check.

We made every new experience into something fun with treats and "yay, this is fun, good boy, good dog" comments in a happy voice. When our friends had a fire truck and police car come to their son's birthday party to visit the kids, we took Jackson to check it out. We let him sniff and see every potentially scary thing in the house, from the vacuum to pots and pans banging, to kids' remote control toys. Today, we are rewarded with a dog who barely lifts his head to check out the fireworks that sound like a war zone each July 4 or during the loudest storms.

We learned that puppy rearing was at minimum a part time job, bordering on a second full time job. Although Jackson was the perfect puppy in so many ways, there were other things where he challenged us and brought me to tears on many occasions.

I learned how patient I could truly be when Jax was teething and learning about which items were his and which were off limits. I watched him like a hawk, following him around most of the time and removing contraband from his razor sharp little teeth, replacing whatever he was chewing with a toy or a bone. He particularly loved the office chair and we lost a few pieces of wood trim on the bottom of it. He also loved coffee table books, and he chewed the spines off of a few books that I had given my husband as gifts. After that, he went to the bookshelves, tearing the spines off of a few of the college textbooks that my husband had saved, which was ironic because the college textbook industry was the industry in which I worked at the time.

Jax was particularly stubborn about learning bite inhibition. We had been taught to give a little yelp in pain like a fellow puppy would do and then remove ourselves from the play session whenever he bit or became too aggressive in his play. With the pain that his razor sharp puppy teeth inflicted, we were certainly not being dramatic when we yelled out in pain. Teaching him not to bite humans was a daily struggle, and I went to work each day with mysterious long welts and cuts down my arms and hands. "We have a puppy," I would tell coworkers who looked at me funny during meetings. "We are working on 'no bite' right now... it's not going that great."

Eventually, though, all of our training and hard work paid off, and by the time fall came and he reached six or seven months, we had the makings of a really well-behaved dog. We took beginner and intermediate obedience as well as some additional obedience courses at our favorite local dog training school.

Before we adopted Jax, I had already started to educate myself on pet food, reading everything I could find, looking up specific ingredients on the Internet, researching brands and other information about canine nutrition. At that time, there were nearly daily stories about contaminated treats from China that made dogs sick. I was learning about food and ingredients and learning that the big name brands that I trusted were not necessarily the best for my dogs, despite the fancy commercials and reputation.

Once Jackson came home I took these efforts several notches higher. I knew the food and treats that we were feeding were safe, and I set out on a mission to ensure that all of the toys that we purchased for him were safely made here in the Unites States by companies that met my strong 'neurotic dog mom' standards for safety and the health our dogs. From toys I expanded my criteria to food bowls, blankets and bedding. We changed our cleaning products and tried to eliminate as many toxins as possible.

In April 2013, our Maggie passed away from Lymphoma. This time my husband joined me in the same room at our vet's office in which I had said goodbye to both Babe and Dutch, both of us snuggling up to our girl. While some dogs do not like to be held too tightly, Maggie lived for snuggling and being held closely, and she had both of us with her when she passed away. We both left crying and headed home to young Jackson whose first order of business after being let out of his crate was to search for his beloved Maggie. His confusion was evident at not finding her and he clearly mourned her, his normal energy level and youthful Labrador antics subdued for several weeks.

Neither Jackson nor I had ever lived in our house without Maggie; she seemed like she should be a permanent fixture in our home. It was too quiet without her frequent hound dog barking, too strange to not have her sweet loving presence with us every day. We had already put down a deposit on another puppy with our breeder, who had become a friend in the two years since Jackson came home, and we were looking forward to being a two-dog household again.

A few weeks later, as Jackson and I walked through the neighborhood, I came across a lawn care service truck spraying an herbicide on the grass at a neighboring home. Jackson and I had started to take twice-daily walks that spring to help him through his time as an only-dog. As I walked home and thought more and more about that lawn care truck and the treatment that it was spraying, I had an ah-ha moment that sent me straight to the Internet. Study after study confirmed my fears that lawn care pesticides have been linked to increasing cancer rates in pets.

After the lawn care awakening I started washing Jackson's paws off after every walk, wiping his entire body and his face down after each outing, and looking for ways to boost his immune system. He was only two years old and Tinkerbell, our soon-to-be new dog, was just a tiny little puppy still in the whelping pen with her mother and siblings. I was going to take every precaution I could to keep both dogs healthy from the very start.

I had gained the 'neurotic dog mom criteria' too late for Babe, Dutch and Maggie, and had trusted everyday big name brands and big retailers to sell me my pet care products. I had walked them through the world without even considering the carcinogenic substances that they encountered in a far more serious way than I did as a human. I had been like so many other loving, trusting good pet owners, but I was going to ensure that I took it to an entirely new level with Jackson and Tinkerbell and their unspoiled "new" bodies. I was going to provide a holistic lifestyle for them from day one, and I have kept that promise to them and to myself.

When Tinkerbell was born, most of my current standards and processes for a holistic lifestyle for my dogs were already in place. We had also just gone through puppy rearing with Jackson and we were much more prepared for Tinkerbell, similar to a second time mom of human babies.

The night before Tinkerbell was to come home with us, we arrived once again in the small town in Iowa where our friend/breeder lives and checked into the same hotel where we had stayed when we picked up Jackson. We had become friends with her over the last two years when we purchased Jackson from her, and like most puppy buyers with the best breeders, we had developed what we knew would be a lifelong relationship with her. After checking into our hotel, we texted her to let us know that we had arrived in town and would be on time for our puppy pickup meeting the next morning.

She texted us back, "Do you want to come have some puppy time tonight?"

'YES, please!" I texted back. I was like a little girl when it came to puppies; I could not wait to throw myself on the ground and let them smother me with puppy love.

Jackson was with us this time and we loaded him back into the minivan and headed off to our breeder's house to meet and choose his little sister. It was his first stay in a hotel and he was loaded with excitement and all of the new smells. Walking him through the hallway to our room reminded me of when I was a teenager and we moved from New Jersey to Indiana. We stayed in a hotel with our Labrador, Snoop, those first few days while we waited for my parents to close on the house and for our moving truck to arrive.

There were two puppies from the litter of seven from which we could choose: Yellow or Purple, as they were temporarily being called based on the color of yarn that identified them. Our friend/breeder was choosing at least one to stay with her and the others were already paired up with their forever homes based on their personalities and the personalities of the other puppy buyers. "I know you like Yellow in the photos but I'd like you to consider Purple, too. She might be right for you," she had emailed us.

Our breeder was an amazing puppy matchmaker and had a gift for knowing her puppies and her buyers and matching them up with their perfect homes, instead of first come, first served like many breeders. Based just on pictures we had our minds set on Yellow puppy because she seemed to be in the thick of things with her siblings, always snuggled up to the other pups and always in the middle of their shenanigans.

"We want this one to be snuggly," we had written, "We want the one who is glued to the others who cannot get enough of snuggling. Whichever one is in the midst of the pile o'pups every day is the one for us!" We were indeed looking for a snuggly puppy this time. Although Jackson is my soul-dog and my best friend, he is loving, but is not overly snuggly. He is getting a bit more now that he is four years old but back then he was rather aloof and preferred to sleep on the tile floor in the foyer rather than on the sofa with us during our evening down-time.

We arrived at our breeder's home and knocked on her door. Just like when we picked up Jackson, we were greeted first by the most gorgeous pack of Labrador retrievers, black and yellow, thick otter tails wagging, body language friendly and welcoming, their athletic bodies wiggling with joy. We greeted our breeder next, this time with hugs instead of handshakes, and chatted for a few minutes.

It was a cool night despite it being July in the Midwest, so we opened the lift gate for Jackson to get some fresh air but left him in his crate in the van. We wanted him to get to see our breeder and the place where he was born but we also were not going to let him run loose with the other intact males, as we were doing a few dog shows with him and had not yet neutered him.

We waited in the yard with excitement while our breeder went to get Tinkerbell's mother, and her puppies. Her mother ran to us to greet us with the same wagging tail and wiggling body as the other dogs, with all seven puppies following behind her. They were big, chunky healthy and happy pups, four girls and three boys, all black, and all so adorable that happy tears started to flow down my face.

Some of the puppies stuck around to sniff us and others headed off to explore. Their mother rolled over onto her back for us to give her a quick tummy rub before going to check on her more adventuresome pups who had wandered off to check out new smells in their yard. I sat down on the grass next to where Yellow was sniffing and reached out to pet her. She gave me a sniff and a little tail wag and proceeded on with her explorations.

I watched her trot off to explore and was sitting there smiling when suddenly Purple puppy came running to me at top speed without any intention of stopping, a puppy on a mission. Purple puppy climbed up in my lap, wiggling so much I could barely get a good look at her, giving me kisses and puppy nibbling my hands. I looked up at my husband, once again tears streaming down my face with joy, and said, "Um, it's looking like Purple might be our girl." He sat down next to me and she launched herself with Labrador enthusiasm into his lap and gave him the same warm and crazy welcome. He grinned widely and said, "Yep, I agree."

"Yellow is sweet but she's been more aloof with us," our breeder explained, "I thought Purple might be more what you are looking for in personality." She was right.

After playing with the puppies some more and making the final no-brainer decision that we did indeed want Purple to come home with us, our breeder took momma and her pups back inside to their part of the house, and we let Jackson out to run around and visit the incredible woman who had paired his father and mother so carefully, arranged for him to come into the world, tended to his delivery and cared for him the first eight weeks of his life. I loved watching their reunion, and I couldn't help but wonder if he remembered that place, if he knew where he was and that this was where he'd been born, or if it was just another place with lots of things to smell. It was one of the million or so times I wished that he could speak English.

The next morning Jackson, my husband and I went back to our friend's farm to fill out the paperwork and pick up Purple puppy who we had decided overnight to call Tinkerbell. Her AKC name would be Faith, Trust and Pixiedust and we could shorten her name to Tink for training purposes to give her that nice one syllable name. Little did we know how much she would live up to her name and become a sweet but feisty and over-the-top silly dog, with a little bit of a jealous streak like the famous Tinker Bell of Peter Pan.

After saying our goodbyes, giving hugs to our breeder and letting her have her own private goodbye with Tinkerbell, we gently placed her in her own crate next to Jackson's crate in the minivan and headed home to Illinois. We had purchased a small puppy-sized crate for her drive home that we would later hand down to our cat as her cat carrier.

As we drove back down the gravel driveway with two Labradors to call our own, I had the feeling that many human moms must have when they bring their second child home. I was not scared of taking care of a puppy this time like I was with Jackson as we had just spent the last two years in puppy mode. My heart was full of love and my mind was thinking about the responsibility of taking on a second life who would need us for everything for the next fourteen or fifteen years if we were lucky.

Tinkerbell whimpered a few times as we drove away, sniffing the air around her and looking around. The sound broke my heart but I was careful not to react or to console her as if she were a human. She had a blanket from her whelping pen with familiar smells, and a giant knucklebone to keep her entertained for the five-hour drive just like Jackson had been given for the journey when he was the little pup. I turned to check on her every few minutes and after just ten minutes of restlessness she curled up in a little ball on the side of her crate closest to Jax's crate and went to sleep.

Halfway home we stopped at a rest area to take both dogs on a potty break. They had met each other at the breeder's house that morning for a few minutes before both going into their crates but had not truly gotten to check each other out. Jackson had never been unfriendly to a dog and since Tinkerbell was just a little puppy, we did not worry that he would try to harm her. However, we needed to be cautious because in his two-year-old Labrador enthusiasm to play with her, we realized he could injure her by accident.

As we led Jackson across the grass on a short walk, Tinkerbell was thrilled to follow along with him. She was not a fan of the collar and leash as she had never worn anything but a piece of purple yarn around her neck before, but she was so distracted by her desire to keep up with Jackson that she quickly forgot about the collar around her neck and just trotted along happily with all of us.

By the time we got home with Tinkerbell and Jackson it was 6:30 in the evening. With the words, "Don't let Jax trample her or hurt her" fresh in our minds from our breeder, we took the dogs outside into our back yard for their first meeting in their own yard. We started off with them on leashes and quickly realized that they were fast friends within minutes. There was no aggressive body language from Jackson, and no fear from Tinkerbell. In fact, she went into play mode with him so immediately and with such energy that we laughed that we had thought it might be the other way around, that we needed to make sure that little Tinkerbell did not trample big sturdy Jackson.

With Jackson as her new best friend, we watched Tinkerbell explore the house with confidence. They have been inseparable since their first day together. The first night she barely whimpered in her puppy crate in our bedroom when we put her in for the night. She could see us, she could see Jackson lying on the floor next to her crate, and she dozed right off.

Tinkerbell was the easiest puppy I have ever raised, at least in terms of house manners. House training was a breeze and she was an overachiever when it came to learning which things were hers and which were off limits to chew. Each time she tested a new item like a shoe or a slipper I told her a firm "NO!" and removed the item from her razor teeth and gave her a toy and told her, "Good girl, yessssssss," as I handed her the appropriate item. Even bite inhibition was easier because she had Jackson to chew on and as a fellow dog, he knew how to tell her that she had bitten too hard.

Obedience class with Tinkerbell was a completely opposite experience than with Jackson. While Jackson was food motivated and 100% focused as long as I had a training treat for him, Tinkerbell didn't care about the training treats and sat and stared at the other dogs, the other people, the ceiling, and the walls. I struggled to get her to make eye contact with me or to even care or participate in any of the training. Eventually, though, she and I passed puppy class and basic obedience school.

Throughout her puppyhood and even now I notice that she looks to Jackson to see what he is doing and will mimic his behavior. We practice their training exercises together and I have watched her looking at him when learning something new, like the "touch" command where we ask them to jump up and touch their nose to our hand. She learned "speak" from watching him, as well as "shake hands."

Although we took Jackson with us to get her so we didn't have to leave him behind and so that he could see our breeder again, I think that her transition into our world was far easier for her than it would have been if she had not had him, an instant friend and dog ally, by her side through all of it. As of this publishing, Jackson is four and Tinkerbell is two and they are best friends, perhaps the most bonded pair of dogs that I have ever seen.

It is amazing and funny to see their differences in personality after coming from the same loving breeder and going through the same training program by the same human parents. Jackson is loving but has a naturally serious expression on his beautiful face which makes us laugh when he does something naughty like steal a napkin out of our hands while we are eating. He is a usually well-behaved gentleman of a dog with a naughty side that comes out when he wants to get my attention by playing "grab Momma's stuff," a game that I accidentally taught him to be an efficient way of getting my attention.

He loves to be petted but follows the strict dog etiquette of not wanting to be hugged or have humans holding him too tightly. He loves to hop up on the sofa next to us and present his chest and neck for a nice long scratch and sometimes does his "upside down puppy" maneuver in which he positions himself for tummy rubs by diving headfirst to the floor and performing a tuck and roll with a half twist to get onto his back. We don't think he realizes that he can simply lie down and roll over.

Tinkerbell is our crazy girl who hurls herself into everything that she does. My husband calls her our "aggressive snuggler" because of the flying leap she will take to land on top of us, followed by a full body stretch and her laying her sleek beautiful face on our chest and staring up at us with her soulful innocent brown eyes, as if she is saying, "I didn't mean to trample you, I just want to lay on top of you." Her eyes are just a slightly brighter shade of brown than most Labradors and there is no way we can hold her clumsy over-the-top affection against her when she gazes at us with them.

Whereas Jackson likes to be loved at a slight distance, Tinkerbell is the dog version of the person who sets up their blanket next to yours on an otherwise deserted beach. She will lie next to Jackson in the same exact position that he is laying, with her body touching his. Or she will run full force into him and knock him off of his feet when she wants to play. Sometimes I find them both in his kennel, the door open and a look on his face that seems to say, "Come on, you've got our own kennel, go hang out in it." I am waiting for the 'No Girls Allowed' sign to go up on his kennel door.

Raising Jackson and Tinkerbell is one of the greatest joys of my life, and it is largely because of them that I can use the knowledge, skills and information that I have learned and honed along the way to teach others how to take their own dog ownership to the next level. They are the basis of the Love, Laugh, Woof Philosophy, and have prompted us to make a healthier lifestyle for ourselves as well.

It is without a shadow of a doubt that I credit losing Beau, Babe, Dutch and Maggie in a relatively short span of time, followed by raising two puppies with their whole lives ahead of them, as the inspiration that shaped my philosophy on dog rearing. They are the reason that I work so hard to provide a holistic and safe lifestyle for Jackson and Tinkerbell. It is what drives me to celebrate these young years and view every day with them as the ultimate gift that a human can receive from another species, which is the friendship that spans our lack of a singular language, our differences and unites us together in love.

CHAPTER 3

DESTINY AND THE LOVE, LAUGH, WOOF PHILOSOPHY

I am very flattered that I often hear a similar message from some of my friends who are not dog lovers. "You have shown me why people love their dogs so much," two different and unrelated friends have told me. This is the ultimate compliment, even more powerful than when other dog owners ask for my input or advice on something dog related. To hear this sentiment from non-dog people means that I have opened their minds and hearts to the joys that dogs can bring to the human world.

As someone who is very active on a variety of social media channels, I see dog posts from other dog lovers all day every day, which include a mixture of silly dogs, cute dogs, adorable puppies and motivational sayings. Those are wonderful and I participate in sharing my own photos and stories of Jackson and Tinkerbell and their antics.

Then there are the other stories. The dogs that are tortured, abused, and discarded like a literal piece of trash to exist on their own in a human dominated world. Sometimes I can hardly bear to see another story or to read another account of a dog being tortured at the hands of someone evil. I want to save them all, every last one. I want to hold them all and let them know that there are loving people in the world who will not do that. I want to pet them gently, feed them treats and help them find their forever homes with good loving humans.

Usually all I can do is share their story through social media with the hope of creating awareness. But in early 2015, I had the chance to actually make a tangible and meaningful impact on one dog whose story I saw online. As a volunteer with Chicagoland Lab Rescue, an all-volunteer group in the Chicago and surrounding suburban area, I saw a request for a foster home for a yellow Labrador named Destiny that would change both of our lives forever.

Destiny had been found in a wooded area of Puerto Rico, tied to a tree by a thin slip lead style dog leash, the type that you see sometimes at the vet's office or a boarding kennel. A plastic bag had been used as a muzzle to secure her snout, leaving her unable to chew through the leash, eat, drink or even pant to cool herself in the hot Puerto Rican climate. Whoever had done that to her had one wish: for this beautiful yellow Labrador to die a slow and miserable death alone and hopeless.

Thankfully, someone who was taking care of some abandoned puppies in the same woods found Destiny. The Good Samaritan who found Destiny ran for help and brought back people to help free her and get her to safety. She was skin and bones, terrified and filthy, but she was alive.

Of course when they found her, Destiny was not named Destiny. Her rescuers, along with Love Puerto Rico Goldens, named her that to help guide her to her true Destiny of living a blessed life in a good home. They bathed her, fed her, got some weight on her and had her spayed. Based on the ragged appearance of her nipples, Destiny had given birth throughout her lifetime to at least one litter of puppies, but probably many more than just one. She was also heartworm positive and covered in scars on her head and her legs.

Love Puerto Rico Goldens, knowing that they do not have the financial or human resources to care for and re-home all of the dogs they find on a daily basis, has partnered with several different organizations in the mainland United States. Once in stable condition, the dogs take their freedom flight in a travel crate in an airplane to a foster home to start their new life in America.

When I saw the request for a foster home for Destiny and I read her story, I jumped at the chance to foster her. We found ourselves at Chicago's O'Hare Airport on a January night, playing beat the clock with a blizzard that was coming into our area. This was going to be my first chance to make a real and lasting impact on the lives of one of those terrified dogs whose photo I had seen through social media.

Destiny's plane landed at 7:30 p.m. My husband had dropped me off at the arrivals area with plenty of time to spare to find my way to the Parcel Pickup area while he went to the cell phone parking lot to wait for my call. O'Hare airport is very strict about not stopping to pick someone up until they are ready and waiting with their baggage, so he was going to wait for me in the cell phone lot.

It felt odd to be at the airport with a tote bag containing a leash, collar, dog treats, poop bags, a bowl and a bottle of water instead of luggage. I sat and waited nervously, suddenly realizing that I was the first person this strange dog would see after her first ever plane ride. As someone who detests air travel, my heart went out to her; it was bad enough knowing what a plane was, knowing my destination, and being in the seating area, let alone having no idea what was going on as she traveled in the cargo area.

There was nobody else in the parcel pickup area at the very end of the arrivals terminal, and it was an odd feeling to be alone in one of the busiest airports in the world on a Saturday night. Behind me, outside the terminal, were three lanes of traffic with cabs, buses, and limos as people shouted and police whistles blew amid a frenzy of human activity.

Finally, a representative with the airline headed toward me with a dog crate on a luggage cart. I stood up and walked toward the desk where I was to sign the paperwork to pick her up. I could hear her tail banging against the side of the plastic travel crate as he got closer and I peered in through the metal crate door and looked into Destiny's scared brown eyes.

I waited with my leash ready as the man cut off the zip ties from the crate that had helped keep the door secure during her flight. I had been prepared for her to not have a collar of her own but she was wearing a pretty collar with red and white hearts on it and a name tag that simply said Destiny.

Once the zip ties were removed from the crate, I opened the door with one hand and grabbed her collar, quickly hooking her to the leash. It never occurred to me until after the fact that she could have been scared and bit me, but it was a risk I would have taken anyway to ensure that I did not lose her. I had brought one of Tinkerbell's harnesses and quickly slid that onto her. The last thing I wanted was for her to slip out of her collar in a completely foreign land. My leash had two hooks and I attached one to her collar and one to the harness as I had often done with my escape artist, Tinkerbell, during her puppy days.

Holding the leash in one hand, I picked up the crate with the other and slid it onto the luggage pushcart that I had snatched up after someone had failed to return it to the cart rack. I called my husband to let him know that he could come get us, and we headed outside.

The weather in Puerto Rico had been 82 when Destiny's flight departed. It was about 20 degrees in Chicago as we walked quickly to the designated dog potty area outside the terminal. I had expected her to relieve herself immediately on the sidewalk but she seemed to know that we were headed somewhere special to do her business, and she walked briskly by my side, extremely alert and checking out the sights, smells and sounds, but sticking right by my side.

Once in the potty area she squatted immediately on the dormant grass and peed for a long time. "Ok, let's go find your foster Daddy," I said as we hustled over to the area where I had told him to get me. Again the oddity of the situation hit me, standing amongst the travelers and their luggage with a strange dog and a giant travel crate.

We had to wait a few minutes, so I finally was able to really pet her for the first time. "Hi, sweet Destiny," I said, squatting down and petting her under the head. Her tail wagged furiously as she let me pet her, but her body was trembling with fear, cold or both.

As I examined her, I noticed small scars all over her face and her body, and I would later learn that she did not have any of her lower front teeth. Her nipples were extended as if she had recently had puppies or simply had so many litters that they had not gone back to their normal appearance.

Snowflakes were staring to fall as the blizzard grew closer, and I realized that this dog was experiencing a tremendous amount of "firsts" in my presence at that moment: the noises, the smells and the snow. I could not imagine what she must be thinking, as if she had flown to an actual other planet, or if at this point she just took it all in stride in a "nothing shocks me anymore" way.

My husband pulled up and we stashed her travel crate in the minivan and put her in our own crate. The crate in which she had traveled had to be sent back to Puerto Rico be used to save other dogs, so we dropped it off at the airline cargo center before heading home with Destiny.

By the time we arrived at our house, there were several inches of snow on the ground and she raced around in our fenced in yard, not sure what to make of this frozen ground but clearly happy to stretch her legs and frolic for the first time all day. I laughed that she was like Queen Elsa; the entire area had gone frozen with her arrival.

During Destiny's first few days with us, she was timid but loving. She loved being petted and getting attention from me, but spent the entire time licking my hand submissively. I could scratch her under her chin and ears and that was it. If I tried to stroke her back or pet her side she would throw herself on the ground with all four legs in the air and lick my hands frantically, as if to say, "I love the attention but I'm scared to death."

She was braver than I expected as she explored her new world. The first few days she raced around the snow, chasing snowballs and learning to run on the ice covered deck and grass in our back yard. However, when we learned that she was still heartworm positive instead of having been treated before coming to us, her playtime came to a stop and she had to be on kennel rest or on the leash inside the house so that she would not run and risk damaging her heart because of the worms in it.

After being treated for heartworms she remained on strict orders not to run or do anything to get her heart rate elevated.

This meant kennel rest for much of the day because when she was out of the kennel she just wanted to play.

The first two weeks of kennel rest went by quickly and between her pain management medications and the fact that you could tell that she felt awful, she slept all day every day, for which I was grateful. I took her outside on her leash many times throughout the day and sat with her and petted her on our living room floor with her leash attached. During those weeks she gradually became more and more accepting of my affection, allowing me to pet her back, her back legs and her stomach whenever she rolled over on her back. Sometimes she sat straight up while I petted her back, and other times she rolled just partially on her side, her pink tongue lolling out of her mouth and her otter tail thumping on the floor.

As Destiny began to feel better, she grew less and less patient with kennel rest, barking when Jackson and Tinkerbell played in the next room and trying to run out the door, her leash stopping her progress before she could go too far or too quickly. I increased her time out of the crate, still on the leash, and brought out my educational dog toys for her to work her mind. When Destiny was out of her crate, I put my own dogs in theirs and so she was able to enjoy frozen stuffed Kongs, play the spinner game in which dogs look for treats by spinning the top level of the game in a circle. We worked on easy commands like sit, down, wait and off, and Destiny discovered a love for moose antlers. She happily lay on the floor gnawing on the giant antlers that I purchase for my dogs.

As the month of kennel rest drew to a close, Destiny relaxed significantly with me. The dog who would not turn her back on me developed a habit of sitting between my feet with her back to me so that I could massage her back and shoulders. If I stopped she would twist her head around and look at me as if to say, "Why are you stopping that?"

One day I fell asleep on the sofa and I woke up to find her curled up behind my legs, her head resting lovingly on my knee. By the time she found her forever home in March 2015, Destiny was my best snuggle buddy in the house. She loved to sleep on the sofa with her head on me, or her entire body stretched out on top of me and she particularly loved blankets and pillows. I cried happy tears whenever she enjoyed sofa time as I thought about what her life had been like out on the streets in Puerto Rico. I felt honored that she had deemed me trustworthy as I petted her or touched her anywhere, without her flinching or throwing herself to the ground submissively.

Like many foster moms, I started to question whether or not we should keep her. I had fallen head over heels in love with her and our bond was so deep I could not imagine letting her go. She was my Velcro dog, attached to me, following me everywhere I went, and my emotions were starting to take over the logical part of my brain that said that we should not have three dogs, that our dog family was complete with Jackson and Tinkerbell.

My husband, though, was adamantly sticking to our decision to let her find her forever home. "There is a family out there who desperately needs her to fill a spot in their home, just like we needed Jax and Tink to fill a spot in ours," he told me repeatedly, "We love her but we don't need her like another family needs her." He also pointed out to me that Tinkerbell had not been acting normally for several weeks. He had noticed that Tink was acting in an aloof manner with me, a notion that I wrote off as ridiculous.

I knew deep down that he was right, but my bond with Destiny was starting to override the logical part of my mind. All I could think about was how much she trusted me, how she had blossomed over being treated with love and kindness and endless patience, how much different she looked physically with a healthy diet and the right medical care.

As we went back and forth on the topic and I tried to change his mind, I volunteered to take Destiny to an adoption event that was scheduled to occur a few miles from my house. As much as I wanted to keep her, I was not going to stand in the way of her finding an adopter. A local open house meant that a nice family from the country or our small suburb might adopt, since I could not picture her as a city dog after a fence hopping incident in which she easily leaped over our three foot high fence.

A few minutes after I arrived at the adoption event, a familiar looking family arrived and Destiny and I greeted them immediately. I quickly remembered that I had met them at a different adoption event earlier that year. I had liked them immediately and was touched at the love they had for their dogs whom had gone to the Rainbow Bridge, including their most recent black Labrador, whom they had lost to cancer.

I think it was the fact that the husband is a pheasant hunter just like my own dad, though, that really made our previous meeting stick out in my mind. There is just something about the love between a man and his bird dog that I understand after a lifetime of seeing my own father and the love he has for his dogs. I don't mean the type of bird dog who lives in a kennel outside with an assortment of other dogs; I mean the type of bird dog who hunts a few times a year, sleeps on the bed and is attached at the hip to his or her human.

They spent a lot of time with Destiny, walked her around the property of the event, sat with her, played with her and petted her. They met the other dogs and spent time with them but then came back for more time with Destiny. They talked to me at length about her background, her time with me, her medical issues and I shared everything that I knew. I shared how far she had come, not just geographically but physically and mentally. "She is a very special dog," I told them, thinking about how those same words from my breeder brought me to my own Jackson when we were choosing him from his litter.

I was elated when they told me that they wanted to adopt her but were going out of town for a few days and wanted to make sure she would be all right with their six cats before completing the adoption. It was a valid concern because I was not sure she knew exactly what a cat was. She had spent a little bit of time with our rescued cat Nala, but Nala has an entire section of the house to herself as a retreat when she needs to get away from our Tinkerbell. I was not entirely sure how Destiny would be with a braver cat.

There was also an issue of timing, since my family was going out of town for ten days for vacation, and Destiny would be going to a fellow foster mom's house while our own dog sitter stayed with Jackson and Tinkerbell. Fortunately Destiny's new family volunteered to be Destiny's puppy sitter while we were on vacation, which would give them a chance to see how she would do with their cats.

The day that I took her there was more difficult than I had imagined. I started crying the moment I began to gather her things to take with her, sobbing hysterically with giant tears rolling steadily down my face as I picked up and folded her special yellow blanket that I had purchased for her as soon as I learned she was coming to me. I gathered her food and her paperwork and took it to my car, barely able to see through the tears. I sat in the driveway with her in the front seat, forcing myself to turn the key in the ignition to take her to their home.

I managed to stay tear-free at their home but when I arrived home without her and put her bowls in the dishwasher for cleaning, I lost my composure once more. I cried until I could not cry anymore, and then my sweet Tinkerbell came to console me. At least I think she was trying to console me by sprawling across my lap so that I could hold her favorite moose antler while she chewed it. "You haven't done this in a long time, baby girl," I said to her, as my husband watched with an expression that said, "I told you so" without actually telling me so.

While my family and I were roaming Walt Disney World and spending time with my family in Florida, Destiny's new family was falling head over heels in love with her. I smiled each time I received a text and photo from them, as they shared with me how much they loved her. They observed how she acted with their cats and consulted with some behavioral experts for tips on socializing the cats with her. Knowing this, I was able to keep my mind occupied by vacation instead of getting used to a home without her in it.

When we returned from Florida I went over to Destiny's new home to process her adoption paperwork, and this time my eyes were dry. I had been counting down the moments all day until I could see her and right away I could tell how happy she was in her new home. She was confident and trusting and relaxed, just like she had been at my house, which told me that things had fallen into place just like they should. As much as I love her and she will forever be in my heart and my soul, she is in the right place. She doesn't need to share much needed attention with big personalities like Jackson and Tinkerbell like she would have in our home.

Destiny has found her forever home in a family of dog lovers who will never treat her badly, never tie her up to a tree to die with a bag around her snout, and never add another scar to her beautiful body. They will never do any of the things that happened to her before she was rescued on that November day. She has been adopted into a loving, safe forever home where she can be spoiled with toys and treats, where she will be petted gently and with love and compassion. She will be tended to with the best care possible, just like every dog deserves as its own destiny. Her forever humans are all hers, and she has blossomed more each and every day with them over the last year. I am fortunate that I am able to visit her sometimes, and my heart fills with love at the fact that she clearly remembers me but then after ten or so minutes, she returns to her owner's side where she belongs.

By fostering and healing Destiny, I realized the elements that all come together to make us good dog owners and companions exist in a mindset and a way of life that I call Love, Laugh, Woof. It is this philosophy that guided me through the care of serious medical issues during my late dogs' medical issues. It is what gave me the strength to let them go to end their suffering, even though my own heart broke. It is what has given me endless patience during puppy rearing of Jackson and Tinkerbell and is what helped me guide Destiny to a better life: Love, Laugh, Woof.

These three concepts are what I believe must be in place before you choose to bring a dog into your life, and must remain in place throughout your dog's entire life. And let me be perfectly clear when I say: bringing a dog into your life is a choice. I think I can safely say that there are few dogs who have pushed their way into a human's home, held the owners hostage, and forced the humans to tend to their every need. Acquiring a dog is a choice and it is one that should be made only if you can commit to it for the dog's entire life.

Love

Loving your dog sounds easy. After all, dogs are cute and wiggly and sweet. Dogs want to please us and make us happy. Who wouldn't love a dog?

Unfortunately, the answer is too many people.

For too many people, "love" is used as casually when it comes to acquiring a dog as it is when they say, "I love that sweater, I love and need that pair of boots." But a dog is not a sweater, it is not something to purchase on a whim and then either return or give away when the whim and the "must have" feelings have passed.

By love, I mean real, true lifelong love. I mean the real love that never wavers when things get hard, the love that keeps you going through sickness and in health, like the words spoken in a traditional Christian marriage vow. When you bring a dog into your home you are making the same vow, "I take you to be my dog, to have and to hold from this day forward, for better, for worse, for richer, for poorer, in sickness and in health until death parts us. I will respect, trust, help and care for you. I will share my life with you."

Sure, you don't have to be faithful to your dog, although you will get the canine inquisition when you come home smelling of other dogs. But all joking aside, dog ownership is like a marriage. It is for better or worse, for richer or poorer, through job changes, babies being born, training and behavioral challenges, income fluctuations, and moves across country. Owning a dog includes through sickness and in health, through vomiting, diarrhea, ear issues, anal glands, liver and kidney problems, cancer, and all other medical things that could arise.

Until death parts us means arranging for their care in case they outlive you, ensuring that there is another responsible owner or with a rescue organization to see to it that they are not sent to a shelter or left to fend for themselves. This means accompanying them through the entire journey of their lives, from the moment they become your dog until the administration of the medicine that will send them to the rainbow bridge. It means staying in the room with them on that final trip to the vet, being strong enough to stay calm and not upset them with your own emotions or leave them with the veterinary staff. It means holding them and lying on the floor with them until their heart gives its last beat so that they know you are with them. It means being strong for them no matter what the situation.

Love means never giving up on your dogs, opening your heart fully to them, and having compassion for the reasons behind their behavior. Real love means never abandoning them in a shelter or leaving them with veterinary personnel when their time here on earth is about to come to an end. Real love means forgiving them when they do something "wrong," and never forgetting that we chose to bring them into our lives, not the other way around. Real love means real commitment from the moment they step that first paw into your life until the last breath they take with you by their side.

Love means being there for the messy times, the sad times, the sick times, not just the fun and games. Love means searching high and low to find a dog friendly place to live if you have to move. It means working with them and getting the appropriate training if a behavioral issue suddenly sprouts up, or if things aren't going well when a new human comes into the family. It is easy to love during the fun and happy times, but through the rough times love is harder. Love is not present when dogs are abandoned by those who did not truly love them or in homes that got them on a whim like purchasing a sweater, instead of making a lifelong vow.

65

Laugh

If there is a way to get through life without a sense of humor, I am
not aware of it! Laughter just makes most situations better, even
the hard ones. Having a sense of humor and having fun with your
dogs makes you an overall better dog owner and a happier person,
whether you are laughing with them or at something they've done.
With two young Labrador Retrievers, I laugh a lot.

Let's flash back to Tinkerbell's puppyhood when she was just
a four-month old pup. We had worked with her for two months on
understanding which of the items in our house were her toys and
which were off-limits. For a young pup, she was doing fantastic.
Let's face it, from a dog's perspective it is not easy to understand
why one furry stuffed object is all right to chew, while the other
is a decorative pillow that is off-limits. Both are stuffed and both
are equally chewable. That dogs are actually able to master the
concept that the items are different amazes and impresses me;
I'm not sure if put in the same situation, I would be able to
differentiate between my dog toy and a child's stuffed animal.

One night I sat on the sofa watching a TV show while Tinkerbell
entertained herself on the floor a few feet away. I glanced at her
every few minutes while she happily chewed her giant moose antler
with her razor-sharp little puppy teeth. Later that night when it
was time for bed I noticed that the carpet right where she had been
laying looked matted down. I bent down to inspect and to try to
fluff it up and make sure it was not wet. We had only had one
accident inside since coming home two months earlier, so I would
have been surprised if she had peed there. She was an A+ student
in the lessons being taught, especially house training.

To my surprise the carpet was neither wet nor matted down;
it was gone. Yes, gone! The mesh was still intact, but the carpet

fibers were gone. While I thought she was chewing her bone, she was actually pulling individual carpet fibers out with her little puppy teeth and had made a golf ball sized bare patch in our carpet, right smack in the middle of the floor!

The next morning I showed my husband what she had done, and I laughed as I relayed the story and took all of the blame. I couldn't be mad, it was my own fault for missing that point where she switched from antler to carpet fiber. I relayed the story to my husband with greatly exaggerated detail of how she was chewing the bone one minute and the next I had missed her using her little pointy sharp puppy teeth to carefully pull the fibers out of the carpet but still leave the mesh. His reply was classic and one of the reasons I love him so much as a husband, a father, and my partner in dog-parenting, "Eh, we want to put down hard wood at some point anyway, right?"

How many puppies would be punished long after a mistake like that when they would no longer remember what they had done wrong? How many puppies end up in shelters because the owners cannot laugh at the situation, cannot laugh at themselves for not watching the puppy closely enough?

Laughing with your dog is equally important. Have you ever noticed your dog's tail go into overdrive when you are laughing and having fun, maybe playing fetch or tug or giggling when they lick your face? They respond to that, they live for that happy sound to come trickling out of our mouths. It is an emotional reward for them, like giving applause to someone doing a live performance.

Dogs like to have fun just as much as we do, and they recognize that human laughter is a happy sound. In fact, according to an article in The Scientific American, researchers in Europe studied MRIs of the brain activity of dogs and found that they have more neural activity when they heard positive sounds like laughter versus negative sounds like crying. You can see that in your own dog without an MRI machine just by looking at their happy faces and relaxed wagging tail when their humans are laughing.

Woof

The Woof part of my philosophy on how to be a great dog owner means putting yourself in your dog's proverbial paws on a regular basis. Woof means being empathetic to the fact that your dog is a dog. Your dog is not a small furry human. Although we may refer to ourselves as pet parents or in our, house Mommy and Daddy, I know without a shadow of a doubt that my dogs are dogs. It would be disrespectful to them to treat them as anything else.

So I treat my dogs like dogs. But that does not mean I treat my dogs poorly. It means I treat them with respect, love and kindness, but I always honor the fact that they are dogs. Because they live in our human world, I am a parent to them in the sense that I set the rules, I keep them safe from harm, I choose their dog food, their organic treats, and I tend to their medical care. I teach and enforce the rules and do all of those things that a human parent would do for their kids.

Treating any animal like an animal should never mean treating it poorly, especially when we have intentionally brought it into our home. It should always mean treating it with respect and understanding of what that animal needs. Somehow along the way, there have been people who confused treating an animal like an animal as treating them badly or as substandard to humans.

However, Woof does not mean that we stop being our dogs' leaders. Woof means being your dog's leader, trainer, guide, and caretaker, and ensuring that they obey your commands because they respect you. Just like leaders in the workforce gain the respect of their employees by being fair, patient, clear and concise instead of yelling, shouting, having unrealistic expectations and unclear instructions, your dog will respect you for being kind, calm and firm without being out of control, loud and scary, or threatening.

When I see stories online of dogs who have been tortured by having their muzzles cruelly taped or tied, dogs who have been dragged by evil humans behind cars, or shot or burned, I realize these people do not know animals are there to be nurtured and cared for with kindness. These criminal, barbaric acts are not what it means to treat an animal like an animal or to treat a dog like a dog. To treat a dog like a dog means to love it, care for it, and cherish the beautiful inter-species friendship that we can cultivate.

By honoring the fact that dogs are dogs, I respect their culture, their body language, their rules for communicating and the way they view the world. It is similar to respecting another country and its culture in the sense that different does not mean lesser. Understanding that dogs are dogs allows owners to give them what they require to be happy and to thrive in our human world.

As a result, as much as I would like them to be with me 24 hours a day and seven days a week, I don't drag them out to blazing hot summer festivals, and I don't take them places where there is something happening that would cause them stress. I don't take them for car rides if I know I have to make stops where I cannot take them. I let them stop and sniff interesting things on our walks, knowing that doing so works their minds and provides them pleasure. I let them see and sniff new objects in our home because I know that they are simply curious and want to be involved in my world and to see what I am doing.

I've learned where it is polite to pet my dogs, and I no longer pet the tops of their heads. I provide them the routine they need, and both physical and mental exercise to keep them happy. I watch and pay attention to their non-verbal cues and how they interact with each other. And finally, I marvel every single day that we have a friendship and a love for each other than spans different species, where we do not speak the same language but we can still communicate, and I know I give as much to them as they give to me.

ARE YOU READY FOR A DOG? REALLY READY?

Dogs and humans have been living together for thousands of years. In fact, a recently discovered skull suggests that dogs may have been living with us as long as 30,000 years ago. That is a long history of a shared bond across two distinct species, one that repeats itself over and over in different cultures and societies. Despite this long history of a shared life together, choosing to bring a dog into your life is not necessarily for everyone, particularly with the demands of life in a modern civilization.

For me, the reason I am a dog owner is simple: I love the company and the companionship that a dog provides. They are my best friends, part of my family, part of my very soul, and that relationship far outweighs any of the downsides of dog ownership. My world feels off-kilter, not quite right, without my dogs. Unfortunately, not everyone knows what he or she is getting into when they get a dog or a puppy. Their adorable faces sway some potential owners, particularly when they are puppies.

Puppies are particularly hard to resist. There is a reason the phrase "puppy dog eyes" exists. Add in their extra fluffy puppy coats, the frequent head tilts and their silly antics, and everyone wants a puppy. This is true even if the potential owner is at the mall just to return that Christmas gift that is too small, and this person has no experience raising a dog, let alone a puppy. It seems those adorable puppies in their baby cribs at the mall pet store overshadow all logic and rationale.

Every dog writer will say the same thing: do your research, do your research, do your research. Research the breed or the mix of breeds; think about whether or not your life is right for a dog. Many people who love dogs as much as I do have made the hard choice to not actually get a dog of their own because they've done the research.

Others jump in head first without knowing the first thing about dog ownership and end up becoming fantastic pet parents for life. And tragically, others jump in and back out, leaving the dog at a shelter or living a miserable life in a home in which they get very little care or attention. Then there are the ones who take in a dog and never love it. Instead they abuse it whether by actively participating in the abuse and hitting it and treating it poorly, or by ignoring and neglecting the dog. I don't understand this type. Perhaps they are swayed by the adorable faces and then just lose interest, which is not acceptable when adopting a living breathing creature.

The Down and Dirty, Literally

So let's talk about the reality of dogs and what it is really, truly like to be a dog owner, no mincing words, no holding back, no sugar coating things, but the down and dirty, sometimes literally. Dog ownership is not all games of fetch and puppy kisses, like happy dog owners make it seem. Yes, those moments exist and they are wonderful, but there is more to sharing life with a dog than that. This chapter will truly dig into the nitty-gritty of dog ownership and what life is really like with that cute puppy that some people cannot resist purchasing on a whim.

The bottom line is that dogs are messy, hairy, time consuming, expensive, needy creatures. They do not have thumbs and cannot help themselves, and sometimes worse, they try to help themselves to things that you do not want them to have. They are 100% dependent on you and need continual training, guidance and attention. More of your life will revolve of them than you ever anticipated.

Gross Things

Dogs are often stinky; they love to eat and roll around in the grossest things. They enjoy disgusting things that you will never understand. They bring you these disgusting things, sometimes alive, sometimes not, and sometimes in between. If you want them to drop the disgusting thing, they don't. If you don't want them to drop it, they do. Either way, you're the one who gets to deal with the gross thing.

Bunnies, birds, turtles, bats, and snakes are among the worst things my dogs have brought to me in varying states of being alive. Sometimes they roll in the gross thing in a behavior called scenting themselves. Other times they eat the gross thing and the gross thing comes back to you in a pile of vomit or requires a trip to the vet. I have fished bugs, clods of dirt, a rotting cantaloupe, pieces of plastic, chewed up sticks and all sorts of other items from their slimy jowls with my bare hands on more occasions than I can count.

Dogs will eat grass, lots of it, and then puke it up on your floors. There will be middle of the night trips outside for upset bowels. You will have a special section under your sink just for pet cleanup supplies. You will have puddles of water and slobber in your kitchen, which you will step in and find yourself with a wet sock. You will have random slobber marks on your clothing from where they laid their heads on you, or muddy paw prints on your pants as you head out the door to work because someone got excited and jumped on you.

Thinking back through my lifetime as a pet owner, there have been plenty of run-ins with gross things, like the bird that Dutch plucked off the fence and consumed, the dead snake that Cinder tried to bring home, and the dead fish and muck that Snoop loved to roll in when we were growing up at Lake Lenape. There was the turtle Beau brought to me that was alive but extremely angry at the joy ride he took in Beau's mouth and hissed at me and tried to bite me as I tried to save his turtle life. There was the small animal that Beau and Dutch killed in my mom's yard when I was dog sitting and the discarded items of food that Babe would try to wolf down on our walks through downtown Valparaiso. Maggie the Basset Hound caught countless rabbits in the yard as well as a bat, and she always proudly tried to bring those treasures into the house.

One morning when Tinkerbell was about six months old, she found a decaying and disgusting cantaloupe that had rolled to the very corner of our fence and that we had not noticed when we were cleaning out our garden from the summer. It must have looked like a ball to her, and at six months of age, her recall was still a work in progress. She thought we were playing a game of keep away and I was completely unable to catch her to get the cantaloupe out of her mouth. Home alone with neither my husband nor any of the kids at home to help it took me several minutes to get the rotting fruit away from her and each time she stopped running from me she was able to gulp down another piece. When I finally got to her there was hardly any of it left.

In the middle of the night, the vomiting and diarrhea started. I woke up sometime after it began. We were outside every hour and between trips outside I cleaned the carpet and ordered a new SpotBot from Amazon in the wee hours of the morning. As soon as the vet's office opened I was on the phone to make an appointment. By the time we made it in to the vet she was just throwing up bile and could not keep even water down.

After receiving fluids and medicine at the vet's office, we headed home with more meds. I spent the next twenty-four hours sitting next to her while she slept. I spent the night on the sofa so we could be as close as possible to the door to outside, all the while worrying about our puppy and not sleeping for more than a few minutes here and there. She had nothing left in her system but had no interest in food or water, which was completely abnormal for our little chowhound. It was a success when she started to lick an ice cube and drink little puddles of water out of my hand in the middle of the night.

The following morning she jumped up, ran to her water bowl, lapped up her water and sniffed around her food bowl, ready to eat and start her day. After our thirty-six hour scare, she was back to her normal self. Her first order of business? She ran back to the garden to see if she could find anything else!

Medical Care and Awkward Situations

As a dog owner you will do things to your dog from a medical perspective that will take you outside your comfort zone. When Tinkerbell was a puppy, she developed an infection near her reproductive and urinary area because she was not taking the time to clean herself property after urinating. I noticed a red rash and took her to the vet who instructed me to use a special medicated soap to clean her in the afflicted area. Not only did I have to thoroughly wash her, but also the soap needed to stay on her for several minutes. And so I found myself awkwardly bathing my young female puppy's reproductive area outside on our deck two times a day for two weeks.

In an equally awkward situation, Jackson developed immense swelling in his testicular area after being neutered and so I was instructed by our veterinarian to hold a warm compress on the afflicted area four times a day for several minutes at a time. And so I sacrificed my soft fleecy microwaveable eye pillow to the cause and sat with Jackson that way until the swelling went down and he recovered from being neutered.

On one occasion, I picked my Babe up from a boarding kennel after a vacation. A happy dog that loved people, Babe sat at the front of the door to the kennel wagging her tail back and forth on the cement floor. After ten days at the kennel, she had rubbed the fur and skin off of the very tip of her tail. When I picked her up they had taped it with athletic tape used for horses. They apologized but said it was just a result of how happy and friendly she was and how excited she was to watch people and dogs going past her kennel all day.

Halfway home the bandage on her tail fell off and she began bleeding all over my car. Once inside the house she wagged her tail furiously and blood splattered in arcs all over my walls, my furniture, and my kitchen cabinets. I tried in vain to re-bandage it. Finally, I went to Walgreens and purchased a variety of bandage options including athletic tape and non-lubricated condoms, which I was able to slip over her tail and tape on to let it heal. Between the looks I received from the cashier with such an interesting purchase along with the double takes of people on the street as I walked her, I grew one step closer to the point of being unembarrassed by anything.

When my late German Shorthaired-Pointer, Dutch, developed a large but benign tumor on his chest, it reached a point in which we had to have it surgically removed. It was so large and on the exact spot on his chest where he laid down, and the skin began to stretch to capacity. In the first few days as the surgical area healed the area continued to bleed and drain, and a t-shirt was not sufficient to keep him clean and dry. It was in a difficult area to bandage, and so Dutch spent several days wearing a t-shirt with overnight maxi pads stuck to the inside, which worked like a charm. I remember changing his pads a few times a day, laughing as I peeled off the backing to the pads, complete with wings, and put them on the inside of the t-shirt, because only dog owners would understand.

Dog Hair

Most dogs shed. A lot. Actually in my home, there is more dog hair than I can adequately find adjectives to describe.

Depending on the breed, count on vacuuming multiple times a week. Your vacuum itself will smell like dog even if your actual dog does not smell doggy. You will empty the canister more times than you can imagine.

People who drop in unannounced will likely see dog-hair tumbleweeds drifting across your hard surfaces if you haven't vacuumed in a day or so. You will wash their dog bedding and take more dog hair out of the washer and dryer than you think could possibly come off your dog. Dog hair is a never-ending cleaning job. You will have dog hair on your toilet seat, in the silverware-sorting compartment of your kitchen drawers, and even in your shower.

You will begin to imagine that you are shedding. You will have lint rollers in every room, in your desk, and in every handbag. You will go to hotels on vacation and find dog hair on your sheets even though your dog is a thousand miles away, you are wearing fresh clothes out of the laundry, and you haven't touched your dog in days.

You will find hair in your shoes, in your shower, in your jewelry box, and in the knit of your sweaters. Someone will purchase a pillow for you that says, "No outfit is complete without dog hair" and it will be true. Before you know it, even that pillow will have dog hair stuck to it. If you have dogs who are different colors, it means that no outfit is safe and you will always have visible dog hair on you. At least when I wear black, the hair is hidden.

You will pull your wallet out at checkout counters and have a dog hair fall onto the counter. You will find dog hair in your meal at restaurants. You will make jokes about wishing you could make money off of dog hair, power the world with it or knit sweaters of dog hair so that nobody ever has to be cold ever again in the world.

Housetraining

During puppyhood you will go in and out of the house at least every twenty minutes while your puppy is awake, at least for the first few weeks. This is because your puppy will need to go outside every time he or she wakes up from a nap, every 15 or so minutes while they are playing rough, at the end of a roughhousing session and every time they start sniffing the floor for a place to go. The first few days home you will likely be outside with them at midnight, 2 am, 4am, 6am. You will be so tired you want to cry. You will go inside and outside, inside and outside, inside and outside, over and over again no matter what the weather is, because inevitably, there will be thunderstorms and all sorts of bad weather at the exact time that your puppy has to go potty. That's if you have planned to get a puppy during the warm weather months. If it is winter, you will have this same routine in snow, rain or ice, you name it. All of this is true unless, of course, you want house training to go on forever. It is really up to you, not your puppy, to make it successful.

No matter how diligent you are, there will be mistakes and accidents. You have to keep your calm and not be angry with your puppy because you are the teacher and they are only as good as the education that they receive. They are, after all, a baby of an entirely different species and dependent on you 100% for the rules of this world and how to do them, all while we speak different languages.

You will need to arrange for potty breaks while you are at work or away from the home. Count on them being able to hold their bladder for one hour for every month of their age if they are sleeping and inactive. This means you will need four potty breaks for your eight week old puppy for an average ten to twelve hour day spent commuting to work, working and driving home.

If you rescue an older dog, there is a strong chance that he or she needs some house training, or perhaps a refresher course on not going to the bathroom inside. In most rescue situations, you do not know the dog's background or where it has been taught to eliminate. You will need a carpet cleaner at the ready and all of the Love, Laugh, Woof patience you can muster.

Training

You will follow your puppy around to keep them out of trouble and teaching them the word "no". You will say "no" more than you ever thought possible. If you add in the "yes" training technique you will say the word "yes" more than you ever thought possible as well. "No" and "yes" over and over in a never ending game of "chew this, don't chew that." No. Yes. Good dog.

You will spend the first six to twelve months training them, for hour upon hour. I've heard it said that it takes 100 hours of training to form a well-behaved pet dog. I once had someone ask me how I keep my dogs from destroying all of my possessions and my answer was that I spent the first six months of their life showing them what they could and could not chew.

Those fun and carefree walks you dreamed of? The ones you see other dog owners enjoying? Those people earned those walks, those mind-meld sessions with their well-behaved dogs. You will spend months walking just a few feet at a time teaching loose leash walking and heel before you get to that point. That book you wanted to read? Sure, when the puppy is sleeping, if you're not using that time to clean, do laundry, eat or do other necessary things. But until your puppy can entertain himself for a bit on his own without chewing the cord to your lamp, kiss your leisure time goodbye.

Your puppy will go through a teething and biting frenzy. Puppies play with each other in a game that is commonly called Bitey-Face among dog owners. Without thumbs or other ways to entertain themselves, they bite and wrestle as part of their play. This is fine with other dogs, but it is not fine with humans. Teaching bite inhibition, which means teaching a puppy that human skin is sensitive and should not be bitten, is a long, long,

long process depending on the puppy. While you are teaching the puppy, you will end up covered in tooth marks, cuts, and scratches from the puppy teeth that are as sharp as razors. Teaching bite inhibition is one of the most difficult parts of puppy rearing; it is also one of the most important to ensure that your little pup does not grow up into an adult dog that bites even playfully.

Your puppy will chew anything that he or she comes into contact with as part of a natural exploration of his or her world. Your puppy will find things that you never dreamed would be appealing, like the base of your office desk chair or the drywall that he can reach with his little snout through the slats of his crate, not that those are specific examples that Jackson did when he was a little pup. Chances are you will lose a few pieces of your physical property to puppy teeth.

Time Thieves & Money Grubbers

You will not be able to leave the house for more than 10 to 12 hours at a time without arranging for a pet sitter. Add the expense of a kennel or pet sitter whenever you want to travel for work, for vacation. For us we pay $50 a day, so add about $500 to your vacation budget whenever you want to go out of town. Our two times a day puppy potty breaks were $15 each during the early days of puppyhood.

Say goodbye to doing things after work like stopping after work for drinks with friends, unless someone is home to let your puppy out. You could pay a dog sitter or stop home first to tend to your dogs, and then go back out to meet with coworkers. If you work full time and have more than a few minute commute, you will have just enough time to run into the convenience store on your way home, because you are playing beat the clock with their bladder, even with healthy adult dogs. When they are seniors you will return to the midday potty breaks that they required when they were little puppies.

You will get up far earlier than you would like, every day of the week, every week of the year that your dog is in your life. Dogs don't know it's the weekend and they definitely don't understand or adjust easily to daylight savings time. They just know that their stomachs are empty and their bladders are full, and both need to be remedied immediately. If you are lucky you will master the art of falling back asleep after you have cared for your dog's needs. You can also add at least a half hour to your morning routine, as you will no longer be the only one who needs attention each day before work.

Veterinary bills, food, treats, toys, bedding and other dog supplies will sometimes clean out your wallet. Dogs are expensive and things happen that are beyond your control. We experienced this with Maggie's back surgery that I talked about in Chapter 1, and again when we had three senior dogs at once, all with different medical issues. For many months it seemed that each time I received a paycheck, I gave it all over to my veterinarian. I rarely leave the vet with less than a $100 invoice even for everyday things like an ear infection or randomly upset stomach.

Senior Dogs

When they are senior citizens you will carry them up stairs, lift them into your vehicle, and pick them up when they fall down. They will require medicines, many additional trips to the vet, expensive tests, medical procedures, and dental work. They may develop incontinence problems that make them feel such shame that you cannot scold them without breaking their hearts. They may revert back to naughty puppy behaviors, as their bodies fail them but their minds are still going strong and they have no way to keep themselves entertained.

Living Arrangements

If you rent your home, you will have the extra burden of looking for dog friendly property to rent. Sometimes you will have an incredibly hard time finding a place to live and have to make sacrifices about amenities or location. When I moved to Illinois, I had exactly two places from which to choose that would allow my Labrador Retriever within a forty-five minute commute to my office. Getting rid of her was not an option and so I opted for a longer drive to work and a more expensive rent than I wanted because it was my commitment to her that we have a place to live.

The Bottom Line

If you do not think you can handle the reality of dog ownership, do not do it. Period. Visit other people's dogs, volunteer at shelters, or find a way to have periodic contact with dogs, but do not get one unless you are fully prepared to be there for life. It is simply not fair to the dog.

This is the life of a dog owner. I love it, it is a regular part of my life, but it is not for everyone. My dogs are forever dogs. I wouldn't want it any other way. The mess, the expense, the "inconvenience," the lack of sleep, the slobber on my pants, the hair nearly woven into my favorite sweater, the doggie nose art on my windows...I cannot imagine my life without my dogs. They are part of my soul. They are a part of who I am.

I have been late for work, taken vacation days to sit by my sick dog's side, or to put one of them to sleep. I have cancelled social plans to stay with a sick or scared dog, like Tinkerbell's first 4th of July when she came home the day before and we weren't sure how she would react to the booming noises of neighbors setting off fireworks. I have had times when I was younger when I lived off of peanut butter and jelly because of an unexpected vet bill. I have searched through dozens of apartments to find the only one that would allow my large dog. I have spent my entire lunch hour driving home to let Babe outside to pee because I knew I had to work late but was new in town and did not have a dog sitter.

I have spent time on the dog poison hotline with tears streaming down my face. I have jumped into disgusting muck because Beau was having a seizure in the middle of the hike in the middle of a stream. I have cried on the floor of the veterinary clinic with my arms around my beloved babies because it is my promise to be with them as long as we both shall live. I have cleaned up vomit, diarrhea, and urine from every type of floor surface. I have been woken up at every hour of night for an emergency potty break and have not slept past 6 a.m. for the last ten years, between senior dogs and then puppies. Just last night, I was jolted awake by the telltale sound of a dog retching as Tinkerbell vomited up a chunk of a fleece toy that she had sneakily eaten when I wasn't watching.

Not everyone goes into dog ownership knowing the honest truth of what is involved and that is one reason why so many dogs end up in shelters, or maltreated and tossed aside like a piece of trash. Not everyone understands the work, the monetary cost, and the dedication that it takes to be a dog owner. Not everyone understands it is forever.

When you take a dog into your home you take on an expensive, time consuming and life long burden in which you are 100% responsible for the safety and well being of another creature for life, anywhere from 10 to 20 years, depending on the breed. It is a huge responsibility, nearly as much as having a human child. It is a unique responsibility as well, one in which you are responsible for them their entire lifecycle from puppyhood through staying by their side as they cross the rainbow bridge. You are the center of your dog's universe. And you chose that role. They had no choice.

I mentioned before that dog ownership carries the same dedication as marriage vows, for better or for worse, in sickness and in health, as long as you both shall live. The difference? If you want to separate from your dog, it cannot be self-sufficient; they cannot just go out into the world alone like a spouse can after a split. They must rely on a kind human to find a new home for them, and those homes are in short supply. There are more dogs in need of homes than humans who can take them, or who want to take them. If you want to separate from your dog, it is often a death sentence, and one that you can avoid by really thinking through if your life is right for the tremendous and amazing privilege of sharing your life with a dog before you get the dog.

The Reward

If you are all right with all of the negatives that I have listed, then you will love the positives. There are so many more positives than there are negatives.

Among my favorites are the sweet loving eyes, wagging tails, and warm greetings when I get home. I love the silly antics, playful spirit, the games of fetch and their uncomplicated friendship and companionship. It is amazing to experience the "us against the world" feeling of being in a friendship that is so close that you do not need words to communicate. It is incredibly special to know that you are forever bonded with a different species and that this amazing animal cherishes you and trusts you like dogs and humans have done for thousands of years.

There are the snuggles, the love in your heart when you catch them dreaming with paws twitching and tails wagging, or the noises and gestures that are all theirs. The look that says to you, 365 days a year, that they love you, that you are their world, their human, and that they too cannot imagine their life without you in the same way that you cannot fathom a world without them. The long walks, the expeditions, the car rides, the memories and happy moments that you create together.

Sure, you are getting up at 6 a.m. and usually sleeping in a completely awkward position because there is a dog paw in your back, but the feeling of love when they lay their head on your leg in the middle of the night is priceless. Seeing that beautiful snout staring you in the face the first thing each day is a priceless gift no matter how much of the blanket your beloved pooch stole in the middle of the night. I would never give up seeing Jackson's beautiful face at 6 a.m. as he nudges me to get up and take him outside, or Tinkerbell's wild enthusiasm to start the day in exchange for any amount of sleeping late.

Yes, you will need to adjust your social calendar, whether you are single, married, and with kids or without kids. Instead of going straight for drinks after work on a Friday night, you will have to either run home and care for your dog before meeting up with friends or hire a dog sitter so your dog is cared for properly. You may have to take two cars to all day kids' events so that someone can run home and let the dog out or leave early to make sure the dogs are fed. You will need to make adjustments throughout your entire life in order to make sure your dog's needs are tended to. If you are like me, though, the pull to come home to your dog will have you leaving the party before the others and scaling back your social calendar so that you have more time with your dog.

I had to lay out the negatives, every last one of them in this chapter. It would be unfair to dogs to do any less. Those cute puppy dog eyes are a blessing and a curse for many dogs, like the dogs who are bought on a whim because the owner is caught up in the cuteness and novelty of a dog, but not ready for the reality of one and then casts the dog aside without any regard for the fact that it is a living, breathing feeling creature whose heart will break once he or she is abandoned in a shelter to fend for him or herself.

If you are ok with the negatives, if you go into dog ownership prepared for all of them, the cost, the mess, the inconvenience, the responsibility of another life, then you are ready for the positives, because when you are ready to be a dog owner the positives make up for any amount of dog hair and early morning potty breaks.

The Compassionate Pet Owner

Along with knowing the downsides of having a dog and determining if you are ready for one is the question of whether or not you understand what it means to be a truly compassionate and fair pet owner? Have you ever thought about what it is like to be a dog? I mean really thought about it in depth. I am not referring to the basic everyday things like chasing balls, eating dog food or any of the day to day things that dogs do; I mean really putting yourself in their place, imagining what it is like to walk in their proverbial paws so that you are ready to make their first days with you the best that you can. This is the Woof in Love, Laugh, Woof, which is an essential component to living your life as a compassionate and fair dog owner.

Unless you were your dog's breeder or the person whose home the puppies were born into, at some point you are a stranger to your dog. When you think about it, everyone in your world was a stranger to you at some point except for your mother and father; it is no different for your dog.

Your appearance, your voice, and your smells were all foreign whether you met your dog when he or she was eight weeks old or if you rescued them later in their puppyhood or adult life. Everything about you and your world is foreign to them, from your car to your home, your yard, your other family members and pets. No matter how happy of a home you are providing, every single experience with you is brand new.

Many new dog owners have no idea what experiences their puppy or dog had before joining them. Were they with a responsible and loving person who started to socialize them early to give them the best possible start to life? Did they come from a puppy mill where they were treated like livestock until they were shipped off to be sold in a pet store? Were they completely unwanted and left to fend for themselves with their mother amongst filth and garbage until a Good Samaritan picked them up? Or is it an older dog with a whole lifetime of experiences under their collar that you can never find out about because we do not speak the same language?

We as humans have a hard enough time understanding each other when we do speak the same language. We get caught up in our own stories, our own circumstances, and our own heads, and sometimes we cannot imagine what another person is going through. Don't get me wrong, I love human beings and I think that we could live in a much happier world if we thought about what it was like to live in each other's world for even an hour, and not in an envious way, but an empathetic way, so we could understand their fears and worries. We become better people that way. And when we can do that with our dogs, we become better dog owners and enter a higher level of being ready to be a dog owner.

One of the most important things to remember as a dog owner is that your dog is not a small furry person. Yes, we love them as our babies and we refer to them as our children. We love them like our children, because they are a part of our family just the same as the humans. But to treat them like children is a disservice to them. We must treat them like dogs in order to respect the fact that they are dogs.

However, treating them like dogs does not mean treating them poorly. Treating them like dogs does not mean that they are less than us in the overall circle of life; it means that they are different than we are. It doesn't mean that we abuse them, neglect them, or harm them. Treating dogs like dogs doesn't mean that we abandon them, leave them behind during emergencies, and cast them aside into kill shelters when things happen in our own lives.

Treating a dog like a dog should mean that we learn about how their minds work, what their specific needs are, what their body language means, what they like or do not like, and how we can respect their culture as dogs and connect with them in the most loving and natural way for both of our cultures, human and dog. It means showing them that we are their leaders, their guides, and that we are fair and loving but also firm and in charge so that they can thrive in our world with confidence and joy.

Putting Yourself In Your Puppy's Paws

Imagine the life of a puppy in the happiest of situations, one who was born into a puppy utopia, with a devoted and loving breeder who breeds strictly out of love of the breed and his or her dogs. They spend the first eight weeks of their lives with their mother and siblings. At first they cannot see and they spend their days nursing or snuggled up to each other with their mother and the breeder there to watch over them.

Over time they open their eyes, start to walk, and then start to play. They have their loving mother to guide them, to nourish them, to keep them safe, and they have each other. Their world is as large as their whelping box for the first several weeks until they begin to go journey into the house and the outdoors. Good breeders help the puppy's confidence by exposing him or her to new situations that aren't too much for their unvaccinated immune systems. Even during their explorations and their socialization, they are always together. They have each other, their mother and their breeder.

The puppies reach eight weeks old and the humans start to come to take them home. One lucky one gets to stay with their mother and the breeder and the others go to loving humans who were carefully screened beforehand to ensure that they will be kind and keep the puppy safe and healthy through its entire life. But these kind and loving humans are still strangers, still unknown, and the puppies are whisked off into a strange world, all alone, without their mother or their siblings by their side for the first time in their lives.

Unfortunately not all puppies come from puppy utopia. Far too many of them are born into puppy mills, to mothers who have given birth to litter after litter and who are sickly and malnourished themselves. The puppies are treated like livestock, not socialized, not loved by any humans, and not treated tenderly or kindly. Some are born in shelters, or to backyard breeders or to mothers who are strays.

Some puppies never know the kindness of a human being until they enter your home, making this new development in which you have become the sole creature responsible for their well being, even more terrifying for them. They want to please you, but they have no idea how and it is up to us humans to be fair and clear when showing our puppies the rules of the house and their new environment. Loving you is instinctive to them, but the rules of the human world are not.

Rescue & Shelter Dogs

Rescue and shelter dogs face an equally terrifying situation when going to their new home. Some of these dogs are being re-homed because their owner passed away, a situation that is hardly ideal but is a picnic compared to what some rescue dogs have endured in their lives. Most of them have been picked up as strays, abandoned as owner surrenders, rescued from abuse and neglect, or worse. Every rescue dog and shelter dog has a unique story, just like we as humans do.

Most adopted dogs have been shuffled around throughout the course of their rescue, which is necessary for their safety and for finding their forever home, but scary nonetheless. Many rescue organizations rely on a network of volunteers to transport the dog, sometimes across the country through convoys of volunteer drivers, and sometimes via airplane by pilots who volunteer their time and small aircraft.

A dog may start its journey by being pulled from a kill shelter in one state, into a temporary foster home, then through multiple drivers on short distances across the country to be transported to the rescue organization's veterinarian. From there, they are picked up by their foster, taken on meet and greet dates with potential adopters, attend rescue events, and ultimately are picked up by their forever family. That is a lot of change for an animal that thrives on routine. These steps are all for the dog's own good, but it is still terrifying and confusing.

Puppies and rescue dogs will adapt and each one will settle into its new surroundings at its own rate, but it is important to understand what they might have gone through and to be compassionate about it, especially if they bark or seem uneasy during the first few nights at home. It will take as short as a few days and as long as several months for their real personality to come out as they become more and more comfortable with you, a feeling that will happen naturally when they are in the home of a compassionate pet owner who is fully aware of the commitment that is required and is ready to Love, Laugh, Woof for as long as you both shall live.

BREEDER OR RESCUE: WHERE TO GET YOUR NEXT DOG

No dog book is complete without a chapter on where to get your next dog and what type of dog to get. The next question to ask once you've decided that you are 100% certain you are ready for a dog and all of the responsibilities that go along with the dog is whether or not you want a purebred dog or a mixed breed dog and if you should adopt a puppy or an adult dog. There are hundreds of purebred dogs and no limit to the combinations of breeds to make mixed breed dogs. So let's talk honestly and openly on how to figure this out on your own.

Personally, I did not choose the Labrador Retriever for my breed so much as I was raised along side them and my personality was shaped around them to the point they are a very part of who I am, my lifestyle, my entire world. In fact, the years between Babe passing away and Jackson coming into my life, my entire day-to-day life was off kilter and not quite right without a Labrador Retriever in it. Of course I loved Dutch, my German Shorthaired Pointer and Maggie, our Basset Hound, very much and in no way were they second-class dogs, but something was simply off without a Labrador by my side.

If you haven't experienced the lifestyle that one particular type of dog brings, or if you don't already have experience with a particular breed of dog or a mixture of breeds, it is up to you to do the research before bringing the dog into your home. If every pet owner did this before acquiring a dog, it would save the lives of countless dogs whose owners took on a dog with needs that they could not or would not meet and who turned their dogs over to a shelter as a result. Of course, if you simply want a best friend and the breed does not matter, there are plenty of mixed breed dogs and puppies in need of a home and they will be just as much your best friend and partner in life as a purebred dog.

Puppy Or Rescued Adults

Having recently raised two puppies in a row, I can tell you that puppies are at least a part time job if you wish to raise them right. For my husband and me, it was a job that we eagerly took on and we now have two amazing dogs as our reward for all of those hours of puppy rearing and training. Puppy training is continual work and minimally includes house training, bite inhibition, socialization, obedience training, as well as the part of puppyhood that doesn't have an official word for it but that I like to call: teaching the puppy not to destroy your home or injure itself.

The first few days of bringing home a new puppy typically go like this:

Day 1: You pick up your beautiful puppy and drive him or her home. Your puppy cautiously explores his or her world, tentatively checking things out and getting the lay of the land. You snuggle and play and immediately start house training. He or she naps much of the day from the mental exhaustion of such a big day, re-energizing that little puppy body so that he or she is wide awake when you want to go to bed.

Day 2: You wake up bleary eyed from multiple trips outside with puppy throughout the night, and immediately take the puppy outside. You bring your sweet little puppy inside for puppy breakfast, which he or she wolfs down hungrily. Fueled with sleep and calories, which you yourself have gone without while tending to the puppy, your sweet little puppy becomes a shape shifting menace, a whirlwind of nonstop activity that you will follow from room to room for the next two weeks, making sure that he or she does not destroy your home or cause harm to him or herself.

Day 3 and beyond: Repeat Day 2.

Of course, some puppies are more mischievous than others, and some breeds are more insane during puppyhood than their calmer relatives of the dog world. However, anyone going to care for a puppy needs to be warned that you have just committed yourself to a long journey requiring patience, time and dedication in order to have a well behaved, friendly and nicely socialized dog.

Your puppy is a blank slate that you are 100% responsible for teaching the law of the land. To not teach them is unfair. The best case scenario for an untrained dog is that he or she, lacking the proper instruction, destroys your most beloved possessions and urinates all over your home and you tolerate it because you love your dog. The worst case scenario is that your adult dog bites someone, causing harm to a human which can result in the dog being euthanized as a vicious dog, you cannot handle the chaos of an untrained dog and you surrender it to a shelter where it is euthanized, or your dog ignores your sit and stay command, runs into traffic and is hit and killed by a car. Neither the best nor the worst scenarios are ok.

Teaching obedience is not just for competition; obedience commands all have a practical and often life saving reasons behind them. Minimally, your dog must understand come, sit, stay and off, although you will find additional commands that you want your dog to understand. This is not just for everyday use but for situations in which instructing your dog to come or stay might save their life, like the time Dutch escaped from our fence and I found him across the street heading down the sidewalk. I gave him the "sit" command and he sat until I could reach him and lead him back to our home. If he had simply run to me, a car could have easily hit him as he crossed the street. "Off" is important for incidents in which you drop something like a pill or piece of food that is harmful to dogs, or in situations in which your dog finds a contraband item.

I once saw a t-shirt that read, "If you don't train me, don't blame me." I agree completely with that; it is our responsibility to teach our dogs how to exist in our human dominated world. Period. I have heard people say, "The stupid dog did (fill in the blank)" and all I can think is that it is not the dog that is stupid, it is the owner's fault for not teaching the dog.

If you are adopting an adult dog, the amount of training you will need to do will depend entirely on the specific dog. Adult dogs need homes for a variety of reasons. Some go into shelters as strays after being picked up loose without any available history of their previous life. Other dogs are owner surrenders from a variety of homes, some decent and some awful. Some adult dogs find themselves in shelters and rescue after their owners pass away, and others are turned over by puppy mills and backyard breeders who no longer have a use for them.

We have had two very different types of rescue dogs in our family. Babe was an owner surrender whose elderly owners both had a sudden decline in their health that left them unable to care for an energetic two-year-old Labrador. Surrendering her to a rescue broke their heart because they loved her very much but knew it was the most altruistic thing that they could possibly do for her. They knew she would be happier with another home.

As a result of their training and care, Babe waltzed into my life knowing all of her commands and with wonderful manners in the home, a nearly perfectly behaved dog. She had a play biting issue and liked to gnaw on my wrist and forearms, so I only had that as a training issue to solve, which I was able to do quickly. I adopted her when she was two and was blessed to have her as my canine best friend until she was 13 years old.

Our Basset Hound Maggie came from a much sadder and more mysterious background. Likely a puppy mill puppy, Maggie was in an abusive and neglectful situation before being adopted by my husband as a two-year-old dog. He named her Maggie May on the ride home after hearing the Rod Stewart song of the same name and set about training her and working through many of her fears over the course of several months. At first she was skittish and had some behavioral issues like nipping at the children. He built her confidence, helped her become accustomed to the three small children and vice versa. He taught them how to act around her, and taught her what it was like to live with love and structure.

When I became part of the family four years later Maggie was one of the sweetest, happiest and most cuddly dogs I had ever met. I was shocked to learn that she had so many issues when he first adopted her and pleased to have found someone who had the same commitment to his dog that I did. When I moved in with Babe and Dutch, Maggie became my third Velcro dog and the three dogs became a little pack as if they had lived together their entire lives.

Regardless of the dog's history, when adopting an adult dog, you should always take at least one round of obedience classes with the dog. Even if your new dog is perfectly behaved in every way, taking a class together is an important bonding experience and a way for the dog to get used to you being his or her leader. Some rescue organizations have a basic obedience class as a mandatory part of their adoption process, but if they do not require it, I can tell you that the experience is well worth it. There is always something to learn for even the most veteran dog owner, whether about dogs in general or about your particular dog.

Adopting through a foster-based rescue organization provides you more information about a dog than going directly from a shelter. The foster family has had the dog as a part of their day to day home life and can tell you how the dog is doing with house training, obedience, what his or her temperament is like, how the dog is in the car, at the vet and in a variety of situations. This is particularly nice for first time dog owners or adopters who have children, cats or other dogs in the home.

Many dogs in foster-based rescue organizations have been pulled from shelters through an elaborate network of volunteers both at the shelter and with the rescue organization. Some rescue dogs are transported from kill shelters in areas with larger dog overpopulation problems as a way to save as many dogs as possible. Adopting a rescue dog may free up that foster home for another dog to be pulled from the shelter.

Finally, some rescue organizations offer a "foster to adopt" arrangement in which you can foster a dog with the understanding that you can choose whether or not you would like to become a "foster failure" and adopt the dog yourself. This is a great way to see how a particular dog fits into your family, especially if you have other dogs at home already. If the dog is not a perfect fit, you can simply help him find his forever home with another family or individual. "Failing" as a foster is one of the few failures that is really a success, and you will join other "foster failures" whose foster dogs came into their lives and never left.

However do not overlook shelter dogs, as there are many amazing dogs in desperate need of homes who are waiting for their forever families to adopt them straight out of the shelter. Adopting directly from a shelter can often literally mean life or death for that dog, particularly if their time for adoption is running out and there are not any hopes of a rescue pulling them. In many instances shelter dogs have an extremely short amount of time to find a home before they are euthanized.

Mixed Breed Dogs

A mixed breed dog is a dog whose parents are different breeds or mixed breeds themselves, resulting in a combination of several different breeds. Mixed breed litters are usually an accident because the owners of both parents neglected to spay or neuter their dogs, although there are increasing numbers of "hybrid" mixed breed dogs in which breeders intentionally blend multiple breeds to bring out the best qualities of both breeds. A popular intentionally mixed breed dog is the Labradoodle, a mating of the Labrador Retriever and the Poodle. If you look through the history of purebred dogs, essentially all breeds are the result of mixing different types of dogs together, sometimes over centuries.

Shelters and rescue organizations are full of mixed breed dogs that need homes, particularly since most mixed breeds are accidents and the owners often do not have resources to take the puppies, or in the saddest cases, simply do not care. Mixed breed dogs come in an unlimited number of beautiful sizes, shapes, coloring, marking and personalities, often making it fun to try to determine which breeds went into creating your unique companion. When adopting a mixed breed puppy, it is sometimes difficult to predict the adult size to which a puppy will grow, but that should only dissuade you if you are a renter and may face a size restriction in your housing contract. In that situation a mixed breed adult dog may be a more suitable choice so that you know how big your dog will be when fully grown.

Mixed breed dogs can be trained to perform many of the same functions, sports and activities that purebred dogs often do, including obedience competitions, agility, dock diving, and other dog sports. They can also be trained for search and rescue work, comfort dogs, therapy dogs and other jobs helping humans. At least one theme park in the United States offers a stage show comprised entirely of rescued mixed breed and purebred dogs performing stunts and tricks in order to promote dog adoption. Essentially, the only activity that is off limits to mixed breed dogs is conformation, which judges breeding stock against the breed standard for that particular breed.

Purebred Dogs

In our world today, most people love a particular breed because of its appearance or personality, but the entire reason that dogs were bred to have certain characteristics was so that they could perform a job. This applies to visual characteristics as well as personality traits.

For example, the big, thick otter tail of the Labrador Retriever that knocks wineglasses off coffee tables and sends knickknacks flying across the room is actually to help the dog as a rudder when swimming in the water. That double coat that sheds so much that the vacuum canister needs emptying numerous times is really designed to insulate the dog in cold weather or cold water to maximize the use of calories; the dog burns calories on the task at hand instead of using them to stay warm. The webbed feet that pick up mud and track them into your home are actually to help the dog swim to retrieve fishing nets and waterfowl. And the keen intelligence and seemingly endless energy that makes them so silly and mischievous actually enable the Labrador to perform jobs like helping fishermen with nets, their original purpose, hunting alongside their humans for water fowl and upland game, acting as guide dogs for visually impaired humans, for assistance dogs for other humans who need their help, and as Search and Rescue dogs[1].

From my perspective, those traits of the Labrador are what keeps me loyal to this breed. I will gladly take the things knocked off the coffee table, the endless shedding and the webbed feet full of mud each spring in order to also have the keen intelligence, the endless energy and the sweet and fun-loving personality. Those

---

[1] The Labrador Retriever Club. "The Labrador Retriever Illustrated Standard." *The Labrador Club. Com.* The Labrador Retriever Club, Inc. 2002. Web.

traits are what make the Labrador so amazing to me, because I love the interaction that we have: their readiness to have fun and play, their love of going for walks and playing outside with me, and their four season love of the outdoors.

For other people, though, the last thing they want to do is run around in the snow in 20 degree weather making snow balls for their Labs to fetch, making up mental games to wear their dogs out during inclement weather, or spending time seeking out pet friendly bodies of water so that their dog can go for a swim just for fun. To me, that is the fun of owning a Labrador.

This is the reason why significant research needs to go into choosing a dog breed for anyone looking for a purebred or mixed breed dog. Too often, puppy buyers are lured in by the adorable faces and they skip researching characteristics of the breed when it reaches adulthood, only to find themselves with a dog that they cannot control or who does not fit into their lifestyle. This is one of the primary reasons for dogs to be surrendered to shelters.

Using the example of the Labrador Retriever, my dogs are not for everyone. I cannot count the number of times I read the comment, "I want one" when posting photos of my dogs when they were adorable little balls of puppy cuteness or now as stunningly regal adults. Of course my photos were when they were sitting sweetly, playing with toys or sleeping. What people do not see from the adorable photos of sleeping puppies is the work that it took to get them to that point. And yes, I say work because a sleeping puppy is indeed an accomplishment, a reward to your hard work of puppy rearing.

Even knowing what I was doing, knowing what I was getting into, I had a few moments when Jackson was a nine week old puppy where I was so exhausted and frustrated after a full day of keeping him from peeing in the house or destroying all our possessions that I had a few epic crying sessions when I wondered if I would ever get to sleep or eat ever again. There were a few days when I calmly put him in his crate for a little nap so that I could step away for a few minutes, have a cup of tea, take a shower, and reenergize myself for the next round of Lab puppy insanity.

When you have a lifelong commitment to your dog and you know what to expect from the breed that you have selected, you get through those moments just as I did, thinking, "This is where non-committed owners would throw in the towel and give-up, but you'd have to wrench him from my dead hands for me to give this dog away. We will make it through this." And make it through it we did, only losing the leg of a desk chair and a little bit of drywall in our family room throughout his insane chewing phase. Can you guess how we survived that part? That's right: we laughed.

Match Making, Doggie Style: How To Research Your Favorite Breed

There are plenty of resources online to research different dog breeds before you choose your dog. The American Kennel club is a great resource as is the TV channel Animal Planet. Both have charts for potential owners to research how easy a particular breed is to train, how much exercise the dog will need, how much grooming is involved, how affectionate the breed typically is, and a variety of other personality and physical traits. Both sites also offer questionnaires to lead to you a few ideal choices of breeds. http://www.akc.org/find-a-match http://www.animalplanet.com/breed-selector/dog-breeds.html

Several great books have been published that provide an overview of different breeds of dogs, including their size, the amount of work that goes into grooming the dog, how easy or difficult the typical dog is to train, and many other breed specific facts. I recommend The Complete Dog Breed Book, The Dog Breed Bible, or the American Kennel Club's The New Complete Dog Book: Official Breed Standards and All-New Profiles for 200 Breeds.

The most important things to keep in mind when choosing the type of dog are their activity/energy level, how easy or difficult they are to train, how easy or difficult they are to groom, and whether or not their size will fit into your lifestyle.

Activity/Energy Level:

Most dogs are at least somewhat energetic; the whole point of having a dog is to have a friend and companion who likes to do things with you. After all, they are dogs, not just stuffed animals with a heartbeat. Matching your own activity and energy level to the dog that you are about to add to your life is critical.

When Jackson was a puppy I saw a post from a fellow Labrador puppy owner while I was reading the latest discussions on a dog forum: "My puppy doesn't ever slow down, how am I supposed to relax and read?" I laughed long and hard at that as I glanced over at the book I had started to read before he came home but had yet to finish. In fact, the only way that I had the free time to be on that forum was because I had earned an evening of relaxation by taking Jackson to puppy kindergarten where he wore himself out by frolicking with other similar aged puppies for 45 minutes and he was snoring away next to me.

Be honest with yourself about how active and energetic you want to be. Many dogs are happy with daily walks and games of fetch in their fenced yard, but some need much more than that.

On the flip side, if you are someone who is on the go all the time, hiking and running and always active, make sure you get a dog who can keep up with you. Don't get a German Shorthaired Pointer if you live in an urban high rise and like to stay inside most of the time. Similarly, don't adopt a low energy breed if you want to hike 20 miles every Sunday with your dog.

Size

As far as choosing the energy level and personality of your dog, it is better to rely on the characteristics of the breed versus the size of the dog. There are small high-energy dogs that are extremely athletic and large breeds that are big couch potatoes who are happy to sleep most of the day away.

If you rent your home or apartment, the size of your dog will probably matter. Most apartment complexes and landlords who offer dog friendly units will stipulate the size of the dog. When I was looking for apartments in Suburban Chicago when I first moved here, the magical number was 60 pounds. My search for apartments that permitted dogs up to 60 pounds yielded exactly two results compared to the hundreds of apartment complexes in the area.

If you rent your living quarters, I strongly suggest not going above a 50-60 pound dog in case you must move and come up against a weight restriction. It does not matter that size has very little to do with how much of a canine footprint you will leave on your rental unit after you move out. Most landlords stipulate a certain size dog and the last thing you want to do is find yourself homeless or in a situation where you have to decide to live on the street or give your best friend away. The 50-60 pound guideline is not set in stone; do your research where you live to see what restrictions typically exist in apartment buildings near you should you find yourself looking for a new place to rent.

Health Issues

If you choose a purebred dog, it is essential to research to find out which health issues are common for that breed. For example, as we learned through our experience with Maggie's back surgery, Basset Hounds, Dachshunds and Corgis often are prone to serious spinal issues because of their long bodies and short legs. Giant breeds can have frequent joint problems and be at greater risk for bloat, while some dogs have higher rates of cancer or other diseases.

Two particular areas to research in terms of breed specific health issues are whether or not the breeder has done health checks and certifications for those issues and if you should take any particular steps to prevent specific issues from happening.

Most responsible and professional breeders have their studs and bitches tested for certain common health problems through the Orthopedic Foundation for Animals (OFA or OFFA). Many breeders have this information in the dog-specific information for each dog in their breeding program. You can also go to the OFFA website at www.offa.org and view a list of suggested tests for any breed that you are thinking of acquiring.

Knowing the breed's frequent health problems helps determine what steps may be taken to prevent issues from occurring. For example, Basset Hound owners should limit the amount of jumping that their dog does to avoid unnecessarily straining their back. With my Labradors, I insist on no playtime for at least an hour after eating in order to avoid bloat. I also do not feed them when they are panting and breathing heavily for the same reason;

instead I wait for them to settle down and get their breathing back to a normal level before giving them their food.

Choosing Your Breeder & Debunking
Some Myths About Breeders

The words "dog breeder" can elicit some very negative responses from individuals in the dog community. The truth is that there are a variety of different types of dog breeders ranging across a wide spectrum of levels of care, and it is neither fair nor accurate to lump them all in together. Some breeders love their dogs as if they gave birth to them, and they put care and love into each litter. Others are unscrupulous and inhumane to their dogs and help contribute to the pet overpopulation problem in two ways: producing more dogs than they have a need for and not sufficiently screening puppy buyers to ensure that they are committed to caring for the dog humanely for its entire life.

Unfortunately, too often good breeders are lumped in with bad breeders, but the fact of the matter is there are many wonderful breeders who operate in such a way that if everyone who bred dogs followed their lead we would not have the heart wrenching pet overpopulation problem that we do in this country and across the world. While I agree with the "don't shop, adopt" concept, it is important to note that good breeders of purebred dogs are important to the world of dogs and to maintaining the breed standard of the breeds that we love so much.

Each dog breed has a set of breed standards created and maintained to ensure that dogs in the breed are bred with the same characteristics in terms of appearance, temperament and the way that their bodies move and function. Dog breeds are registered with national and international kennel clubs and a breed specific parent club that is part of that kennel club maintains the breed standards. For example, the American Kennel Club is the largest kennel club in the Unites States of America and the most well known. The Labrador Retriever Club is the parent club of the Labrador Retriever in the American Kennel Club, and it maintains the standards for the qualities that each and every Labrador Retriever should have.

Dog breeders should strive to breed Labradors whose mind, body, temperament, and movement align with the breed standard. Breed standards are about much more than just appearance. The breed standard is not just a set of guidelines for dog conformation shows, in which breeding stock is judged according to the criteria, but to ensure that all dogs of that breed are created with the right temperament and body to lead a healthy, happy, and productive life.

Here is an example of a breed standard taken directly from The Labrador Retriever Club website that describes the general appearance of a lab:

> The Labrador Retriever is a strongly built, medium-sized, short-coupled, dog possessing a sound, athletic, well-balanced conformation that enables it to function as a retrieving gun dog; the substance and soundness to hunt waterfowl or upland game for long hours under difficult conditions; the character and quality to win in the show ring; and the temperament to be a family companion. [2]

[2] Labrador Retriever Breed Standard." *The Labrador Club.* The Labrador Retriever Club, 31 Mar. 1994. Web. 31 Mar. 2016. <http://www.thelabradorclub. com/subpages/show_contents.php?page=Breed+Standard>.

Breed standards go into much greater detail when describing the individual makeup of the dog. Here is an example also from the Labrador Retriever Club website that shows how breed standards work to ensure that the dog is well suited to the job for which it has been bred:

> Neck - The neck should be of proper length to allow the dog to retrieve game easily. It should be muscular and free from throatiness. The neck should rise strongly from the shoulders with a moderate arch. A short, thick neck or an "ewe" neck is incorrect. Topline - The back is strong and the topline is level from the withers to the croup when standing or moving. However, the loin should show evidence of flexibility for athletic endeavor.[3]

Unfortunately there are many breeders who do not breed to the standard, resulting in a wide range of Labrador appearances and temperaments. Breeders who do not breed to the standard are doing a disservice to the breed and even more so to the actual dogs who can suffer from genetic health issues as a result. This typically happens to the more popular dog breeds. Using my Labrador example again, the Labrador Retriever has been the most popular dog in the United States since around 1991.[4]

---

[3] "Labrador Retriever Breed Standard." *The Labrador Club.* The Labrador Retriever Club, 31 Mar. 1994. Web. 31 Mar. 2016. <http://www.thelabradorclub.com/subpages/show_contents.php?page=Breed+Standard>.

[4] Boccone, Bud. "America's Best Friend: The Labrador Retriever." *AKC.* The American Kennel Club, 19 July 2015. Web. 31 Mar. 2016. <http://www.akc.org/learn/akc-gazette/americas-best-friend-the-labrador-retriever/>.

For diehard Labrador lovers, this is not good news because it means that anybody with unaltered Labradors can mate them, create a litter and have a good chance of selling them. However, not just anyone should breed dogs, and not all dogs should reproduce. Using my Jackson as an example, he is a stunning dog who meets the breed standard. His mother is a hunt test champion and his father has had incredible success in the show ring. I showed Jackson in a few conformation shows before we neutered him to see how he would do. However, when we discovered he had several seasonal allergies that plagued him, we chose to neuter him so that we would not risk passing those allergies into an entirely new bloodline of dogs. Not all owners will do that or consider the dog's impact on future generations of dogs.

There are essentially three types of dog breeders who bring purebred dogs into the world: Large Commercial Breeders, Backyard Dog Breeders and Hobby/Professional/Show Breeders. Some may separate hobby breeders into a different category than professional breeders, but I think of them as similar enough to put together.

Large Commercial Breeders

Large commercial breeders breed and house puppies in a manner similar to raising livestock: in large quantities in cages. These operations are often known as "puppy mills" because they breed puppies in large quantities. The level of care can dramatically vary and there are many horror stories of puppy mills in which dogs are undernourished, dehydrated, and kept in cages too small that create physical problems. It is not uncommon for puppy mill dogs to never touch grass or get to run around and live a normal life prior to adoption.

Several years ago when I wrote the blog for an international organic dog food company, I interviewed the owner of a small Chihuahua named Furby. Furby's back is forever hunched because his cage was too small for even a little five-pound dog. He lost all of his teeth and part of his jaw because the only water that he was given was through a hamster cage style bottle and he never drank sufficient water to rinse his mouth, and he was kept in cages full of females so that he could continually produce liters of puppies.

Most large commercial breeders sell their puppies through pet stores. Because of the lack of attention to care, genetic issues, temperament, and socialization, many puppy mill puppies have substantial health issues and are harder to acclimate to your home than a puppy from a loving and caring breeder. Adding to this problem is the fact that most pet stores do not fully screen buyers sufficiently or not at all. This means that puppies can be bought on a whim as easily as a pair of clearance boots.

Puppy mills and pet store sales create a terrible and never ending Catch-22 of wanting to save the puppies for sale in pet stores while also not wanting to give them business and promote additional puppy mill puppies from being bred. It is a tragic cycle of how to stop the demand without putting the supply in harms' way. What happens to the puppies and breeding stock if nobody purchases them? The consequences can be deadly for the dogs. Dog lovers have spent decades protesting puppy mills and pet stores who sell purebred puppies from large commercial breeders, and there is still an incredible lack of awareness on these dogs' plights with the general public.

Some puppy mill operators will partner with rescue groups who take in and re-home former puppy mill breeding stock, which is how little Furby was placed into a loving home for his senior years. Others are shut down by local authorities after investigations of abuse, and rescue organizations aid in finding homes for the dogs with people who are committed to teaching them to trust and be part of a household instead of a large breeding operation.

Backyard Breeders

The term "backyard breeder" typically refers to people who breed their own dogs but do not offer the same health guarantees and health checks as Hobby/Professional Breeders. Some backyard breeders will breed just one litter because they have a beloved female dog and want one of her puppies to keep for their own, or because a friend or family member wants one of her puppies. In this situation, it is quite possible that the parents and puppies are well loved, quite healthy, and receive the utmost care and socialization, and will be wonderful dogs for the puppy buyers.

Other backyard breeders are less scrupulous and breed their dogs for profit without the same high quality care and treatment. Backyard breeders who fall into this category often neglect their dogs and simply view them as a way to bring in income, similar to puppy mill operations but on a smaller scale.

When choosing a puppy from a backyard breeder you should always visit the home before committing to a puppy, to see the living arrangements for the mother and puppies. Dogs should be living in the home with the owners or in kennels that are clean, climate controlled, well maintained with plenty of fresh water, fresh bedding and room to move. All of the dogs on the premises should have an overall well cared for appearance and temperament.

Hobby/Show/Professional Dog Breeders

Professional dog breeders, sometimes called hobby or show breeders, are my preference of breeder for purebred puppies. These breeders breed for love of the breed and usually possess extensive knowledge of genetics, their bloodline, and common health problems of the breed. They are dedicated to maintaining the breed standard in all areas: health, appearance and temperament.

Professional breeders will ensure that all of their stud dogs and dams pass the standard tests for their breeds with the OFFA, also called the OFA, which is the Orthopedic Foundation for Animals. For example, with the Labrador Retriever, you should look for breeders who test for hips, elbows and eyes.

This type of breeder also is usually involved in conformation shows, which judge breeding stock against the breed standard and award winning dogs points towards titles such as Best of Breed, Best in Group and Best in Show. Also look to see if the breeder participates in common sports and activities for the breed. For example, the breeder from whom we purchased Jackson and Tinkerbell is actively involved in Hunt Tests, Conformation, Obedience and Agility, works professionally as a dog trainer and runs a boarding kennel in her community. Some breed multiple litters a year and rely on that income, and others breed just once or twice a year or when they would like to add another dog to their kennel or home or to produce a batch of puppies from specific parents.

Other things to consider with a professional/hobby/show breeder:

1. What is the application process? Good breeders will require an extensive application to be submitted to ensure their puppies are going to homes where they will receive appropriate care, socialization, training, affection and exercise.

2. Does the breeder have a lifetime return policy? This means the breeder will take the dog back at any point in its life and dictates that the owner is not to surrender the dog to a shelter or rescue under any circumstances. By choosing a breeder who makes this stipulation in your purchase contract, you have chosen someone who truly cares for their dogs and is committed to keeping them safe.

3. What health guarantees does the breeder provide? What is the policy in the event of a disease such as hip dysplasia in a Labrador whose parents have gone through the correct health tests? Breeders should guarantee the puppy you purchase should be free of genetic defects. Of course, few people could really truly take a dog back to the breeder for this reason but some will offer to pay part of the veterinary bill or a discount off of another puppy, if the health issue proves to be fatal.

4. What type of registration will the puppy have? Is the breeder registered with the American Kennel Club? Many breeders choose to only sell puppies with Limited Registration, meaning that the puppy is a fully registered purebred dog within the American Kennel Club, but the kennel club will not register their offspring. This

is designed to help control the breeder's bloodlines and prevent overpopulation and unauthorized litters. Limited Registration is often accompanied by a contractual agreement that you will spay or neuter the dog within a designated period of time.

5. How many litters does the average female produce? Look for breeders who do not over breed their females. Females should have active and happy lives with other activities besides having puppies around the calendar. Also look for breeding programs that use males from other breeding kennels so that other bloodlines and genetics are continually being brought into the litters of puppies.

Hobby and show breeders love their dogs and their websites will usually include pages of their males and females with photos, temperament descriptions and brag pages with the titles that they have earned. Look for breeders where the demand usually exceeds their supply; they will be worth the wait to get a great puppy. Additionally, you can sometimes adopt grown dogs that may have been returned to the breeder due to owners passing away or for other reasons. The best breeders will sometimes direct you to various rescue organizations or other breeding programs if they believe that will be a better fit, or if they will not have any puppies available in the timeframe that you desire. Many breeders are active supporters and volunteers for rescue groups; they do not contribute to the pet overpopulation problem with their own litters and they work hard to make sure that homeless dogs find the right homes.

When you choose the right breeder, you will know it and develop a lifelong relationship with him or her. My breeder had tearful goodbyes with each of my dogs when she said goodbye, even though she knew they were going to a great home. She had helped deliver them, helped their mothers care for them and started to socialize and train them to prepare them for the biggest adventure of their lives: going to their forever home.

The discussion of rescues versus breeders, puppy mill breeders and backyard breeders is often a sensitive one because dog owners who have purchased a puppy from a less than desirable situation are often defensive that their dog is just as wonderful as other dogs. It is important to remember that dogs who are born into puppy mills and bad backyard breeder situations are just as deserving of love as those from rescues or reputable professional breeders.

The controversy is that by continuing to purchase from these sellers, a demand for their product is perpetuated. With reputable professional breeders, the demand usually exceeds the supply; it is when the supply of puppies exceeds the demand that we have a dog overpopulation problem, combined with a lack of criteria for puppy buyers who purchase from most backyard breeders and pet stores, and a lack of the Love, Laugh, Woof lifelong vows and commitment.

Without a puppy buyer evaluation process like the best breeders mandate, puppies and dogs can end up maltreated and abandoned, creating the heartbreaking situation that we have in our country. Professional reputable breeders are frequently blamed, along with puppy mills and backyard breeders, with creating the problem, but the reality is that they are as passionate about controlling the number of dogs being born as any rescue organization. Blame might also be placed on the owners who purchase a dog regardless of where they purchase it and do not have the lifetime commitment, the Love of Love, Laugh, Woof, the dedication to the dog from the first meeting until the final breath as a senior dog.

LOVE, LAUGH, WOOF AND
SURVIVING PUPPYHOOD

Love, Laugh, Woof starts as soon as you bring your new puppy home. You selected your puppy out of love and you have committed to giving your puppy the best life possible from the first day until the last day of his life. Of course puppies are insane, to put it bluntly, and a mixture of love and laughter will get you through his or her antics, as well as a heavy dose of woof to try to put yourself in the puppy's position.

Puppy rearing is not for the faint of heart, but you can and will survive and raise your puppy into a fantastic dog if you put the required work and dedication into it. Training your puppy begins the first night home and includes house training, obedience, bite inhibition, and teaching your puppy the rules of the house in terms of which are her toys and which things are off limit.

The First Night Home

Woof means putting yourself in your dog's position and having empathy regarding the dog's new situation. In this way, you can meet your puppy's needs and be a caring and compassionate dog owner. Let's think about what it is like for puppies when they leave their mother and littermates and go to their forever home by using my Tinkerbell as an example.

On July 3, 2013, Tinkerbell woke up like she always had, with her mom and seven siblings, part of a silky black pile of cuddling puppies that had slept together since they were in their mother's womb. She ate her breakfast and played with her littermates in their whelping pen, just like normal, perhaps hoping that they would get to play in the blue plastic puppy pool or explore the edge of the pond with their mother and their breeder.

Mid-morning, her breeder came to get her and brought her into the main part of the house with the big dogs. Shortly after that, there was a bustle of activity and all of the big dogs ran to the front door with her following behind to see where they were running.

We walked into the house and greeted all of the dogs, petting them and saying hello, and Tinkerbell wagged her tail as she remembered our smells from our initial meeting the day before. My husband and I both picked her up and held her as she gave us puppy kisses all over our faces. As we filled out paperwork and chatted with our breeder, who had become a friend since we had brought Jackson home from her two years prior, Tinkerbell went back to playing with the other dogs in the house without a clue about what would happen next.

When it was time to leave, we put her new puppy collar around her neck, appropriately decorated with Disney Tinker Bell figures. It was the first collar she had ever worn and she tossed her head around, confused by the feel of it around her neck.

With her new collar on her neck, we placed her into a crate inside our minivan, all alone without any of her siblings, whom she had spent the last eight weeks snuggled against. There was a big strange dog in the crate next to her along with us, the two humans she did not know who were now calling the shots instead of her mother or the breeder.

That she whimpered just a few times before curling up into a fox sleeping position is incredible; I would have screamed and cried in protest if I was in her situation. I would have banged against the kennel door and made my displeasure known. That this little puppy would just take it all in stride seemed miraculous.

Imagine being a child and being removed from your mother, your siblings, your toys, your home, and being taken from all that is familiar by someone you don't know. Now imagine that there is a language barrier preventing you from communicating. Add in an entirely new set of rules in this new place. How do you feel so far? Bewildered? Terrified?

Not every puppy can have an instant canine friend by its side when he or she goes to a new forever home like Tinkerbell has had with Jackson. She was able to see him do things first and learned from Jackson they were safe and not scary.

However, it was not just Jackson who made her transition from life with her littermates to life in our home a positive experience; it was our understanding that this could be very scary for a puppy. Not every puppy has understanding owners who understand the Woof, who understand what the puppy has gone through.

And finally, not every puppy has the utopian experience that Tinkerbell had for the first eight weeks of her life. If your puppy is from a puppy mill, backyard breeder or abusive background, he may have been maltreated, bounced around from place to place, not socialized, not introduced to new things or had any of the great early life experiences that our Tinkerbell had with her breeder.

No matter what a puppy's start to life is like, those first few days in the new forever home are critical to establishing your relationship and setting him or her up to be confident, happy dogs. When I talk about the Woof part of the Love, Laugh, Woof philosophy, Woof is putting yourself in your dog's position, thinking like a dog and embracing the fact that he or she is a dog.

On that first day and night home, you know that your dog is in a loving home. After all, you've prepared for her arrival, you've counted down the days, and you are going to love her for the rest of your life. However, your puppy has no idea about any of this, especially that first night after she's sniffed the new smells, explored the home, eaten new food, and is on her own for the first time in her life, away from her littermates and mother. She does not know that you have loved her since you met her. All she knows is that everything she knew has changed with zero warning.

Let's take the example of bedtime. How many owners have tucked the new puppy away in its new crate and been awake all night with the puppy howling, crying and barking while they wonder why the puppy will not just sleep quietly? How many have gotten annoyed at the puppy because she will not settle down and just sleep through the night after several days in the new house? How many have been upset because the puppy had an "accident" in the crate overnight?

Speaking honestly, if I was that puppy, I would be howling and crying too, after finding myself all alone in a strange place, the first night away from my comfortable family of siblings and mother, away from the humans who had started to gain my trust over the course of the day. You would hear me miles away as I cried in utter despair to be let out, to have some company, as I wondered what had happened to my world without any sort of explanation.

Embracing the Crate

After raising two puppies in two years I have developed some tips on making your puppy's first few nights home a success. We followed these guidelines with both Jackson and Tinkerbell and actually got some sleep those first few weeks.

There is sometimes a debate about crates, with some dog owners adamant against them, calling them cruel. Yes, if you lock your dog in your crate as a punishment, or for most of their lives, and ignore the dog and deprive the dog love and attention, a crate is definitely cruel. But that is cruel behavior no matter where you put the dog. If you lock your dog in the bathroom for most of its life, it is equally cruel, or put them on a tie out or in a doghouse. Anytime you confine your dog to too small a space or deprive him of love, affection, human contact and exercise, it is cruel. If you leave your dog home alone all the time without any attention or anything interesting, that is cruel. The crate itself is just an object, a tool. It is how you use it that makes it humane or cruel.

When crates are used correctly, they become a dog's haven like our bedroom is to us: a place to relax and maybe even escape from the activity of the rest of the house. In my home, we joke that we want to take the crates out of our bedroom, but the dogs like them too much and like to curl up in them sometimes throughout the night. We compromised and took one crate out and left one. Sometimes I will wake up in the middle of the night to hear the crate door banging against the crate and I will find Tinkerbell using her nose to bounce the unlocked door open to let herself in. I often find both Jackson and Tinkerbell in their other crates with the doors wide open, both napping even though they have their choice of any sofa, dog bed or human bed in the house.

When your puppy or new dog comes home and you are going through your list of things to purchase, I strongly suggest buying two crates, one wire crate and one hard plastic travel crate, both in a size that will fit your adult dog comfortably. We use large wire crates when we leave the dogs home alone and a plastic travel crate in the bedroom. This has worked perfectly because when we need to use the travel crate for actual travel we can just move it to the car and then back into the bedroom since most of them are lightweight enough for the average person to wrangle, even for large dogs like our Labradors. If you really want to be prepared and not have to move crates around, buy a third crate, another plastic travel crate that you can keep in your garage or your vehicle.

When your dog is a puppy or when you bring home a rescue dog, position one crate in your main living area where you spend the majority of your time, whether as a single person, a couple or a family. No, it's not your ideal decorative item, but trust me on this. You can move it once you get to the point where your dog only stays in the crate when you are gone. Put the other crate in your bedroom next to your bed. It will be an eyesore, too. It's ok; it's not going to stay there forever but it is important the first few nights and up until you can trust the puppy not to get into mischief while you sleep.

The First Week

Put a soft towel or small blanket in the crate in the bedroom where your puppy is going to sleep. If you brought something home that smells like the previous place, put that in the crate. Keep it folded up puppy size for your new pup to lay on, but don't spread it out throughout the entire crate, as you don't want it to be able to absorb any urine during the night.

A half hour or so before your bedtime, play with your puppy or new dog. You can work on a new and simple command like "sit," or allow some playtime with new toys. Even little puppies are usually happy to play a game of fetch or chase the ball. Using the brain will tire the dog even faster than physical exercise.

After your play session, take your dog outside for one final potty break before bed and allow a small drink of water. Take the dog to your bedroom and put him in his crate, using the word "kennel" or "crate," whatever word you have selected to identify the space. Give a tiny treat as you shut the door and get into bed. Your puppy or dog should be able to see you from the crate and know that you are still there.

If your puppy or dog cries or whines, tell him "quiet" in a low, calm, stern voice. It is important to make sure that you are not saying this out of anger or saying it out of frustration, but simply speaking in your calm but stern training voice to get your pup's attention.

If the puppy or dog is still crying after ten minutes, he might need to go to the bathroom. Very patiently take him outside and give him the chance to urinate or defecate, bring him inside, place him back into the crate with the crate command, and lay back down in your own bed. Give the "quiet" command if the puppy or dog resumes crying.

You may be forced to let the puppy cry a bit, but the crying should stop faster than if he were in another part of your home because he can see you and know that you are there. You are sending the message that you are there, you will take him outside if needed, but that his place is to sleep in the crate.

Know that your puppy will likely have a legitimate requirement to go outside a few times throughout the night. The first week with both Jackson and Tinkerbell, we had multiple puppy potty breaks throughout the night, but neither had any accidents. At first we went out at 10pm, midnight, 2 am, 4 am and 6am. The second or third week we were down to one potty break around 2 am and after a month they slept through the night. It is normal to go outside multiple times throughout the night with a very small puppy. When your puppy is small, their bladder is small.

A general rule of thumb is that your puppy can hold his or her bladder for one hour for every month that they are old. At eight weeks, or two months, this is 2 hours. Just like us, they often can go a little longer when sleeping, but it is unlikely that you are going to get a full night of sleep the first few weeks that a puppy is home with you.

Other Crate Times

The wire crate in your regular living area is where your dog will stay when you are not home or not able to watch him/her until you can trust that your puppy will not get into mischief when left alone. Puppies explore the world with their mouths and no matter how much puppy proofing you do before bringing your new family member home, your puppy will find things to try to put into his/her mouth that you never dreamed possible. Use the crate when you take a shower or run out to get the mail especially during your pup's first few months at home. You can also use the crate during family mealtimes unless you can wear him out before you sit down to dinner.

Make sure you purchase a wire crate in the correct size for your adult dog. Choose a crate with a removable wire divider so that you can restrict the puppy to part of it when he first comes home during house training. You want the puppy to be able to move around and change positions while sleeping but not have so much room that he can urinate or defecate in the crate and move far away from it. The reason for this is not cruel; it is to help teach your puppy that the crate is not an acceptable place to relieve his waste. As the puppy grows, move the divider to increase the kennel size, and remove it entirely once the puppy is house trained.

Place a small blanket or towel in the crate for a little cushion once your puppy seems to be mostly housetrained, but do not spread it out throughout the entire crate as it can be detrimental in house training because beds and blankets absorb urine. It is not something cruel, it is to help with your house training efforts. Once your puppy is fully house trained without accidents, you can add the fluffiest most comfortable bed that you can find.

The crate in the main living area can be used when you want enforce puppy naptime. Just like human kids, puppies can become over tired and extra naughty. Using the crate so you can catch a breather is perfectly all right. It's important to say again that a crate is never used as punishment, but puppy rearing is exhausting work and it's better to give a little nap time than to get frustrated and take it out negatively on the puppy. Chances are he/she will curl up quickly and go to sleep when he is in the super hyper puppy mode.

Just like human kids, I found that my dogs both became extra naughty when they were overly tired. Even going by Labrador Retriever puppy standards, extra naughty means extremely over-the-top crazy puppy behavior, not normal puppy playtime, so a little downtime in the crate kept my sanity while they rested their bodies and brains for the next play session.

It is important to remember that the crate is for the puppy or dog's safety to keep him out of things that can be harmful. When used correctly, your dog will come to view the crate as a safe and comfy place for him to relax. Crates should never be used as punishment or to lock the dog up so he/she is out of sight. Owners who do so should simply not have a dog. Crates are exclusively for use for the dog's safety to make sure that he/she is not chewing the electrical cords, jumping up and turning on gas stoves, destroying the furniture, or any other behaviors that puppies or newly adopted adult dogs could discover when left on their own.

When you are home with the puppy and not sleeping or in the shower, you should have your dog or puppy out of the crate with you, allowing you to interact with each other as you have fun, train, exercise or rest together. Puppy rearing will definitely take the place of many other activities and hobbies that would typically fill your time so plan accordingly and know that the majority of your non-working, non-sleeping time is going to be spent with your new family member outside of the crate.

The First Few Days

I strongly recommend taking vacation time from work the first week of your dog or puppy's arrival home, like a canine maternity leave. I did when Jackson was a puppy and it was a lifesaver. If you share your home with another adult, you might even take back to back weeks of vacation so that you have two weeks to get your new dog used to her or her new world, particularly if you are starting with a puppy or if you have a rescue dog with special needs or an abusive background. In terms of puppies, between late night potty breaks and the limited amount of time your puppy can hold her bladder, you will be happy you did. Similar to a new human mother, when Jackson napped, I did laundry, cleaned, read, or slept. When he was awake we played, bonded, and worked non-stop on housebreaking.

Usually on the first night, your new puppy will be exhausted and somewhat reserved as he explores his new home. Enjoy that night, because it has been my experience that in the next few days, the dog's personality will wake up, his sense of adventure will come out, and you will have your hands full of puppy antics. Of course, personality and your puppy's energy level is the entire reason that you chose your particular dog. It is exactly what you knew you were getting into with a puppy, but even with all of those factors, even with your Woof attitude strongly in place, with Love strong in your heart, the Laugh bubbling to the surface, it is still sometimes exhausting and utterly frustrating those first few days with your puppy.

It is important to remember that your puppy's entire life is influenced by those first few days at home, and this is not the time to introduce it to stressful situations. It is not the time to bring them to a parade, to your 4th of July fireworks, to the family picnic or to meet the neighbor's dog. No matter how many people want to come and see your puppy, the first few days are for exploring your home and getting to know you, the humans, in a calm and positive environment.

Tinkerbell came home to us on July 2, 2013. We live in a subdivision in suburban Chicago and our neighborhood literally sounds like a war zone. Between the bright lights, the flares, the flashes, the thundering booms, they could re-film the Burning of Atlanta scene from Gone with the Wind in our subdivision each Independence Day.

Knowing that Tink's first few days with us should be calm, quiet, positive and non-scary, we had a master plan for making sure she was not terrified of fireworks for her entire life. And so on July 4, my husband and the kids headed off to fireworks and I stayed behind with the dogs. Around 7:30 pm I woke her up from a sound sleep and engaged her in play, rolling the ball to her, working on "sit" and teaching her name, letting her explore the yard, introducing a new dog toy to the toy bin. I did a dance of joy when Jax started a game of Bitey-Face with her, and by 8:15 our little puppy was sound asleep, crashed on the sofa next to me snoring lightly. Success!!

With the puppy asleep, I turned the AC to a cooler setting to ensure that it kept whirling away, I turned the TV on for background noise, I added a box fan for additional background noise, and I settled in for Tink's long nap through the festivities.

At 9 pm it was nearly dark and the first fireworks in the distance began. My husband texted me, "How's it going?" and I answered, "Perfect, she's crashed, sound asleep."

By 9:15 the neighborhood was celebrating in full force, loud booms going off every second from different directions. Jackson raised his head up and looked at me, then resumed his evening nap, since we had worked to make sure he was not afraid of fireworks or storms during his puppyhood. I settled in to take advantage of the sleeping puppy and began to read my book as the festivities erupted outside. And then she woke up.

Our rule during house training is that the puppies must go out immediately after waking from a nap. I watched as Tinkerbell stood and stretched her little puppy limbs, stretching into downward facing dog and then a stretch forward. I waited for a moment hoping she would just turn around and find a new position. Instead she waddled over to me, wide-awake.

I picked her up and carried her to the back door with Jax following behind me, always ready to go outside. Outside it sounded like the world was ending, with M80s going off, smoke bombs, and seemingly professional quality fireworks. I put Tinkerbell on the deck and she stood and looked around and trotted down the steps to the grass. As she squatted and peed and I praised her with the normal "good girl" praise, she looked around calmly at the insanity that is 4th of July, and without missing a beat trotted off with zero fear to go see what Jackson was up to. And so I found myself outside on July 4th with both of my dogs who didn't even notice the loud booming noises, with all of my fears of the day traumatizing her completely unfounded.

House Training

House training was the part of puppy rearing that terrified me the most when Jackson came to our home. I had never had a puppy of my own and the last one that I helped house train was my parent's dog Dutch, who I puppy sat for several weeks when he was still going through house training. That had been thirteen years before.

Because Jackson came from a professional breeder, she had started working on house training already. From his first moment home, we worked hard to have as few "accidents" as possible, taking him outside immediately upon waking up, before going to bed or into his crate, and every few minutes during intense play sessions when he was running around. Each time he relieved himself outside we heaped joyful praise on him and gave him treats. The few accidents he had inside we caught immediately while he was in the act and told him a firm "no" and then picked him up, took him outside for him to finish, and then praised him.

Within weeks, we were accident free and by the time he was four months old we declared him fully house trained. We did have one misunderstanding when he noticed some bushes next to a long bay window and while smelling the bushes through the open window and screen he lifted his leg. We are certain that he got confused about whether or not he was inside or outside because of the proximity of those bushes, and he hasn't gone inside our house since.

We practiced the same techniques with Tinkerbell and she was a quick study at house training just like her big brother, house trained at just a few months old and without accidents with the exception of a urinary tract infection when she was six months old. In fact, we set a goal of no accidents for the first few weeks and were pleased to have just two small accidents during her puppyhood. Neither of them ever pooped inside the house during puppy training.

House training requires immense dedication to teach your dog as quickly as ours, and not everyone will have these results. Taking vacation time to be at home with a new puppy will help. Do not lose your Woof mindset and get frustrated with your dog if he does not catch on as quickly as Jackson and Tinkerbell. Just make sure you put in the work and the dedication; having a beautifully housetrained dog will dramatically reduce the stress level for both you and your dog.

The Importance of Training & Socialization

Your puppy is a blank slate when he or she is born, a tabula rasa, as they would say in Latin. It is our responsibility as humans to train the puppy or dog to know what to expect and how to behave in a human dominated world. Training is part of the love, the lifelong commitment to giving your dog the best life possible.

If we do not train dogs to know the rules, we cannot blame them when they behave in a way that we do not like. Without training, dogs live a stressful life in which they frequently get in trouble but do not understand why, sometimes moving from one undesirable behavior to the next in a whirlwind of wrong behavior and either negative reinforcement or punishment.

Training and socialization are what make a dog a pleasant member of the family. Training means showing your dog how to act when given commands, both vocally and visually. Socialization means introducing your dog to a variety of people, other dogs and experiences in a positive way so that he is not afraid of those things when encountering them later on in life.

When people fail to do these important things, they fail their dogs and set them up for a lifetime of doing the wrong thing, getting in trouble and having a life that no dog should ever have. When you train and socialize your dog, you are your dog's hero, his best friend, and you set him up for a lifetime of knowing how to behave, what to do to please you, and how to feel confident and happy in his role as your best friend.

Training your dog covers a variety of areas of your dog's life. It is not limited to commands like sit, stay, and down, although those are more than just something taught in obedience class; they are literally potentially life saving skills for your dog. Training includes how to act when meeting new people, experience with meeting new dogs, how to act in the home, how to walk on leash, and where to eliminate their bowels or bladder.

No matter how much I love my dogs as if they are my children, I know that they are animals. Yes, they are tame and domesticated animals, but they are animals. And so they should be taught to go to the bathroom outside, to greet people without jumping on them, and to not bolt out the door, because those are the skills that I need them to have to live in our house.

One of the reasons that training and socializing your dog is so important is for its own safety. Commands like sit and stay, along with a reliable recall (come, here) can literally save your dog's life depending on the situation. Teaching your dog to sit and wait when someone comes to your door could be the difference between your dog living a long life or bolting out the door and in front of a car or getting lost or stolen. Not coming when called is equally serious. If someone leaves your fence gate open you want to know that when you call your dog back to you that he or she is going to come no matter what distractions are present.

When owners fail to socialize their dogs they can end up with dogs that are scared of everything and everyone. And unlike humans who can retreat or protect themselves in a variety of ways, dogs are limited to retreating or growling or biting. This can put the lives of humans, other dogs, and your own dog in danger. The last thing you want to do is put your dog to death because he bit someone.

Owners who put the time and commitment into training and socializing their dogs have a more pleasant experience with their dogs and are less likely to give up and surrender the dog to a shelter or rescue group. It is also more pleasant for the dog. How would you like to start a new job and not have anything explained to you and have to endure your boss scolding you, being unhappy with you and punishing you each and every day before giving up and firing you? That is no way to live for a human and no way to live for a dog.

It is our responsibility as dog owners to teach them and give them the life skills that they require to live as a dog in a human run home. Dog life skills may sound a little odd, but they need to know how to act in a variety of situations. Do you want to spend your evenings coming home to urine on the floor, torn up possessions, dogs who are wild and unruly and do not know how to act, or do you want to come home to your best friend whose mind is melded with you and who greets you with confidence and a wagging tail? The choice of which dog welcomes you at the door is up to you. I can tell you which dog your dog wants to be.

Although it is possible to "home school" your puppy, I am a proponent of attending group obedience classes. Search for a small independent obedience school and instructor in your area. Your local independently owned healthy pet food store is a good resource for such a place, as is your veterinarian. Often, the first class for puppies is a puppy socialization class, which typically consists of mostly playtime with other similarly aged puppies. This is a great treat for your puppy, who might miss the puppy play with her siblings. It is also a wonderful way for your dog to continue to learn the etiquette of playing with other dogs, including dogs that are not their littermates.

After puppy class, I suggest attending a basic obedience class, where you will learn things like sit, stay, down, come. Even as a lifelong dog owner, I cannot tell you how much I learned from my trainers when I took first Jackson and then Tinkerbell through classes. I found myself taking them to additional classes whether they needed them or not, simply because I was enthralled with the information we were learning. In a classroom environment, your dog will learn these commands with the distraction of other dogs nearby. Having a great "stay" is easy in a controlled environment in your living room. Add in ten other dogs and then you have a challenge.

After you learn basic obedience you can continue to take classes to perfect leash walking, learn "off" or "leave it", and learn to "stand" which helps during weigh-ins at the vet. Most dog training schools also offer training on greeting other dogs and people on the street, door manners at the front door, and table manners when the humans are eating.

After the basic skills for the dog's safety, the owner's safety and general comfort around the house are mastered, you can move on to fun activities like agility, competitive obedience, lure coursing, and other fun dog sports. Some classes teach tricks and fun games for you to play with your dog. You can also continue with your dog's training and test for the Canine Good Citizen certificate, which consists of several tests to determine how your dog behaves in a variety of common circumstances.

Bite Inhibition

Without hands and thumbs like humans have, dogs do not have as many options for playing and communicating as humans do, leaving their mouths to do the heavy lifting in many ways, including playing with fellow dogs and with their humans. However, in the human world, we are not as open to a dog's biting, nipping and grabbing us with their teeth, so it is our responsibility to patiently teach our dogs the rules of the human world when it comes to biting, just like we must teach them the other rules of sharing our lives together and bonding across species.

Once again this falls under the love and the woof: love and commitment to making sure they have a clear understanding of how to use their mouths in their shared existence with humans, and putting ourselves in their position and understanding how very different this is from how they interact with other dogs.

There are a variety of ways to teach your puppy not to bite humans; no matter which method you use, it is critical to be fair, consistent and patient just like with any sort of dog training. Always remember that dogs are doing a normal behavior in their own culture and teaching "no bite" is often a time consuming process.

When puppies and dogs play together and one bites too hard or becomes too aggressive, the bitten dog will remove himself from the play session, sometimes after yelping audibly. This is one technique that you can use when teaching your own dog or puppy. Of course, we laughed when our puppies were little that it was sometimes a quite heartfelt yelp of pain that escaped our mouths, as puppy teeth are razor sharp and surprisingly painful for such a small creature. Whenever the pups would bite a human, we yelped in pain, removed our hand and turned our back to remove ourselves from the play session. This was usually quite effective, although some puppies can get to the point of being so over stimulated or so involved in the play session that they just bite your foot or ankle and do not take the clue that you do not want to play.

If your puppy tries to chew your hand, feet, arms, legs or clothing out of boredom, make sure you have an appropriate alternative toy to give to them. This is also true if they are chewing on your chair leg, your purse strap, or your favorite shoes. Tell them "No!" in a firm, stern and deep voice, and then hand them their toy or antler and say, "Yes, good dog!" or whatever your affirmation phrase is in a pleasant and loving voice.

Bite inhibition is a particularly important area in which you should train your human children and sometimes the other adults in your house as much as you train the dog. We spent hours telling our kids, "stop wiggling your fingers in front of the puppy's face" and watched constantly to ensure that they were not teasing the dogs with their fingers, not trying to play rough with the puppies or doing any other behavior to encourage the dogs to bite.

Looking back, I think the kids were harder to teach than Jackson and Tinkerbell, but our efforts were well worth it. Your dog might have the best intentions by play biting, but the risks are too great if you do not teach him that it is not all right to bite humans. A playful nip from a tiny puppy is one thing, but a nip from a 70-pound Labrador could lead to your dog being put to death for being aggressive.

Make sure you speak with your obedience school trainer about bite inhibition, techniques for dogs who are resistant to simple methods, and the concept of soft bite versus no-bite. Your obedience school trainer should have substantial information and guidance for you on the topic that will serve to alert and educate you on bite inhibition as a concept.

A Tired Puppy Is A Good Puppy

One of the best things about puppies is that they are high energy, fun loving, and inquisitive. One of the biggest struggles of puppy rearing is that they are high energy, fun loving, and inquisitive.

Even the most dedicated, loving and prepared puppy owner needs a little break from puppy rearing once in awhile, whether it is to take a shower, eat their own meal or just sit down for a few minutes. Fortunately, although it may seem like puppies could power your city with their energy, the fact is that they need their sleep to grow between all of the playing, exploring and investigating that fills their agenda.

Giving your dog physical exercise is essential, but so is mental exercise. A short training session will work your puppy's mind and wear her out much more quickly than a longer session playing fetch or tug-o-war with her favorite squeaky toy. You can teach simple commands quite young; Jackson and Tinkerbell both learned how to sit and wait for their food at just six weeks, before either even came to our home.

As your puppy learns the sit and wait command you can expand that into my favorite puppy tiring game: hide and seek. Hide and seek is as simple as putting your dog in a sit and wait position and hiding in simple spots like around the corner of a wall or behind a chair or piece of furniture. It may take several tries to get your dog to wait without having eye contact with you, but eventually he will understand and you can become more and more elaborate with your hiding spots. Make sure you praise him happily and enthusiastically when he finds you.

As the years go on you can continue this game, continuing to work on their skills of sitting and waiting even when they cannot see you. I work on it weekly with my dogs; they have fun and so do I. It is also practical in case we are ever in a situation in which I need them to sit and wait while I go somewhere they cannot see me.

Puppy Rearing Is an Extended Process

The most important thing to remember when raising a puppy is that it is an extended process. It is the proverbial marathon and not a sprint. Different breeds take different amounts of time to go from crazy puppy to incredible dog. The first six months should be the hardest with the razor sharp teeth and the tiny bladders that go along with the territory, but that doesn't mean that at six months old you will automatically have a well behaved adult dog in your home. It takes patience, training, love, and then more patience and training and then a bit more patience.

Puppies are not for everyone. As much as all of my friends ooh-ed and ahhh-ed over Jackson and Tinkerbell on social media, I know that many of those friends would have been miserable raising them. We put in countless hours of work to raise them into the awesome dogs that they are today, and even with my commitment and my knowledge of what we were getting into, I still had moments where I had to calmly place the puppy in his or her crate and go and have a good cry in the other room before continuing on my day.

I see so many young dogs surrendered to shelters because the owners did not know what to expect when they brought home that high-energy breed as an adorable little puppy. I am thankful for breeders like my own who do extensive screening and owner education before sending a puppy home to ensure that the buyers know what is involved, understand the lifelong commitment and the work that is involved.

One of the problems with puppy mill puppies and pet store puppies, aside from the horrific living conditions, the inhumane treatment of the dogs and the presence of genetic defects, is that those stores do not ensure that the buyer is prepared before sending the puppy home with them. These are many of the purebred puppies who find themselves in shelters at just eight months old because they were too much dog for the owner to handle, too much work and commitment for a busy family, and so those adorable puppies end up euthanized, their lives wasted and terminated at a young age because nobody told their owners the stark reality of raising a puppy.

Of course raising a puppy is certainly fun and rewarding if you can handle the responsibility and challenges and have the patience to see it through. Puppies are fun and lovable, too, and at the end of a long play session there is nothing sweeter than your little pup falling asleep on your chest or in your lap, especially a large breed who won't fit in the crook of your neck for naps for very long. I loved picking up Jackson and Tinkerbell when they were that little, knowing that in six months that they would weigh seventy pounds. There are very special moments during puppyhood that only happen once, like puppy's first snow, the first time they use their "big dog" bark instead of their little puppy bark, or the first puppy tooth that you find. I still remember the first time that Dutch went on point over a leaf blowing across the grass and the first time that we took Tinkerbell swimming. Those moments are precious and well worth the hard work of raising your puppy into a great adult dog.

LOVE, LAUGH, WOOF, RESCUE

Every single rescue dog is different in terms of background, training, and the positive or negative experiences that shaped him or her into the dog that they are on adoption day. Some rescue dogs are owner surrenders from otherwise loving homes, situations in which the owners just could not afford or find housing with their dog or from a life where their owner passed away. Other rescue dogs are from abusive or neglectful situations and need extra patience, training and understanding. Regardless of the dog's background, it takes considerable time, as long as several months, for any rescued dog to feel comfortable in her new home and to really open up and reveal her personality.

Regardless of your dog's background I highly recommend taking a basic obedience course even if your dog has an understanding of basic commands. Your dog cannot talk or tell you his or her story, and obedience classes are as much about bonding with your dog and getting your dog used to following you as their trusted leader as they are about teaching your dog a specific skill. Even if she knows all of the basic commands, taking a class will also provide a place to train your dog with the distraction of other dogs, a new environment and plenty of foreign smells. It is one thing for your dog to listen to you in your home, but an entirely different matter for your commands to compete with the many distractions in the world.

By taking a basic obedience class you can also have additional conversations about other challenges that your dog may have, particularly if she came from an abusive or otherwise challenging past. Even dogs from the most loving environments might have habits that were all right with the previous owner but that you do not find acceptable. For example, my Babe had a habit of play biting or mouthing my arm to try to play with me, so I patiently trained her to stop initiating that game and instead bring me a toy for a nice game of tug-o-war.

During class, your trainer might notice specific behaviors and suggest a training plan to work on those issues through one-on-one sessions or additional classes. Taking an obedience class also gives you access to a professional dog trainer so that you can ask questions or talk about things that you have noticed at home, so that together you and your trainer can help your dog overcome that past and to feel comfortable and confident in her new life with you. That relationship is crucial so you have someone to reach out to later on if behavioral issues arise later.

House Training

Just like with obedience, your rescue dog's house training knowledge will vary wildly depending on his background. Some dogs, like Babe, waltz into your home perfectly housetrained, while others have lived outdoors and were never taught that it is not an acceptable behavior to eliminate their waste inside a home or building. Other dogs who have spent considerable time in shelters or other confined spaces might be confused about having access to grass or dirt, preferring concrete because they believe that is where they are supposed to go.

The concepts for house training older dogs are the same as a puppy, consisting of positive reinforcement, consistent rules that the dog understands, and patience, patience, patience. Just like with puppies, I strongly suggest crates for rescue dogs. They help with house training when you are not home as the dog is less likely to go in the more confined space of a crate than if she has full run of the house. Crates are also critical for the overall safety of your dog who is just as likely to find things in the house to consume that can hurt them as a small puppy would be. The last thing that you or your new rescue dog want is for her to finally find her forever home and then accidentally turn on the gas on the stove from a bad counter surfing habit. The crate will keep your dog safe when you are not there to do so.

Helping Your New Dog Be Confident

We've talked about the Woof in Love, Laugh, Woof meaning that you think of what it is like to be your dog, putting yourself in their position. Most rescue dogs are bounced around from place to place, particularly those who go through rescue organizations instead of shelters. Some travel hundreds of miles through a network of volunteers who drive the dog for a hundred miles before transferring the dog to the next volunteer. Others, like my foster dog Destiny, fly to their foster homes, and some are stuck in shelters or in boarding kennels while waiting for their forever homes. All of this is necessary to save them. It is done with gentleness and love, but it is still confusing and scary all the same, particularly since the dogs may not have any idea that they are being rescued or that their lives are about to be saved.

You may love your new dog instantly, and know that you are going to keep him close to you until the day he passes to the rainbow bridge, but your dog just knows that he is in a new place yet again. Your dog may even go through a few days where he seems subdued and depressed as he acclimates to the new surroundings.

Once again the solution is to Love, Laugh, Woof. Love is your commitment to your dog's success and happiness. Laughter is needed for some of the silly antics or situations you might encounter, like Destiny's reaction to the snow covered ground that waited for her after her flight from Puerto Rico. And finally, Woof, your compassion and patience and consideration of how you would feel in a new situation, like if you were abandoned in a prison and then shipped to a new land where you do not know the language or culture or the intentions of those around you and in control of you.

Dogs thrive on routine, so it is important to establish your dog's new routines from the start, including feeding time and location, bed time and location, understanding which are dog toys and which items are off limits like shoes and children's toys, whether or not they can snuggle with you on the sofa or on the floor and where they should eliminate their bodily waste. Dogs want to please and they must know your expectations in order to thrive in your household. It is impressive how quickly your dog will adapt to your schedule and lifestyle. Jackson and Tinkerbell know precisely when it is time for a meal, time for play, and time for napping. It was incredible to see how quickly Destiny started to learn our schedule after she became our foster dog.

Praise is important in building your dog's confidence. "Good dog" or "good girl" in a pleasant and happy tone of voice is a great reward for anything that your dog does correctly, even if it is an everyday mundane behavior like laying on their bed. When your dog chooses an antler to chew or lies on their dog bed you can praise them with "good dog" to ensure that they know that they made a good choice.

The flip side of praise is a firm "no" to correct them. A short simple "no" gets their attention more than screaming and yelling. I have found considerable success with my foster dogs using the same method that I used with our puppies. For example, when Destiny chose my shoe to chew instead of a dog toy I gave her a firm "no" and removed the item from her mouth and then handed her a dog toy and said "yes, good girl!" After just a few times she understood which items were for dogs and which were off limits, and I was able to teach her in a way that was matter of fact and she was always rewarded with a good result. Screaming at a dog, yelling at a dog, or hitting a dog is always off limits.

Bonding With Your New Dog

The whole point of having a dog is to have a best friend, a companion, and doing things with your dog will help him understand that you are his friend and that things you do together are enjoyable and safe. Some things, like snuggling, may take more time, but walking, playing and training are great things to do from the beginning.

With a new rescue dog you have limited knowledge on what he is like on a leash, so take precautions in case you have an escape artist. A harness is more reliable than a regular collar because it is harder to escape from. Start off with short walks around the block and venture out a bit more and more with each walk. Changing up your route will give your dog new smells and work his mind with each new route. If his leash behavior is less than desirable, you can work on that together in training class.

Training is a great way to bond with your dog. Not only are you establishing yourself as the leader and easing his stress level as you teach what is allowed and what is off limits, but training is fun, particularly when it involves treats. Make sure you enroll in a training class within the first few weeks of bringing your new dog home.

I still have training sessions with Jackson and Tinkerbell most days, short little rounds of sit/down/sit or speak and shake hands, just for the fun of it. Of course, the most important and potentially life-saving commands of stay and come should be mastered, followed by sit, down, stand heel and off/leave it. After those, though, you can train many of fun things like shake and speak. My husband has taught our dogs to do "touch" and "downward dog" and is currently working on "speak" in another language. They know that "bed" means to go to our master bedroom and that when the tornado siren goes off to run to me.

Playing with your dog helps ease his stress of acclimating to his new home. Fetch is a nice option while you get to know your dog's personality, but use caution when taking the ball from his mouth since you do not know how he will react when you try to grab something from his mouth. The correct way of playing fetch is for your dog to drop the toy by your feet in front of you or to place it gently into your hands.

Avoid aggressive games like roughhousing or tug-o-war at first as you learn about your dog and how he acts when he gets excited or over-stimulated. You do not want either of you in a position in which a bite could happen.

Dog toys are a must with grown dogs just as they are with puppies. Your dog will be more relaxed with things of his own to chew or chase. You can also try interactive toys that you can stuff with food or other treat toys, as well as games where the dog searches different contraptions for treats. Just make sure that you never leave any dog of any age alone with toys to avoid a choking hazard.

Too Much Too Soon

Sometimes it's difficult to take your time getting to know a new dog. As dog lovers, we love every dog and want to throw ourselves into playing and snuggling with the dog. But the last thing you want to do is to push too hard or move too fast and stress your dog out so that she snaps or bites because she was not ready for as much affection as you wanted to give.

When Destiny arrived at my house, I knew her story and had studied her photo for days while I waited for her flight from Puerto Rico. I loved her before I saw her. All I wanted was for her to lay her beautiful head in my lap and feel secure. However Destiny is a dog, not a person, and she had to go through her own process of figuring out that I was safe. It took us a month and a half for her to snuggle with me. When she finally trusted me enough to lean against me and put her head on my thigh I wept happy tears.

It is important to train children and teens that no matter how much they instantly love the new dog, they cannot smother her with affection or hug her right away. This is often extremely hard if they've grown up around other dogs that tolerate overly affectionate people. I learned this the hard way as a child, although it was not with a rescue dog but with my grandfather's dog.

I lived with our incredibly patient Labrador Retriever, Snoop, who had no sense of personal space and laid on top of us and allowed us to hug and kiss her as much as we wanted. When I tried to do this to my grandfather's dog, I got a good nip on the face after I startled her with a big over-the-top hug. Luckily she didn't break the skin and I didn't tell anyone, but I did file it away in my mind not to hug any dog other than my own and only if his or her body language said that it was ok.

No matter what the dog's background, make sure all of your kids know to touch the dog nicely, to not pet too hard, to not run over and hug her, to not lay on top of her or take things from her mouth or put anything in her mouth. Use caution and make sure your new rescue dog is not alone with small children until you are 100% confident that the situation is safe for them to be together without an adult.

Behavioral Issues

When behavioral or emotional issues become evident it is important to find an experienced professional dog trainer to guide you through a solution. Many dog trainers are extremely involved in rescue and have rescued dogs of their own. Your trainer can help you determine if a group class or a series of private sessions is the best option for you and your new dog. Your veterinarian may be able to offer suggestions on training methods or suggest trainers.

To find a great dog trainer, you can utilize a variety of resources. The Association of Professional Dog Trainers has a search tool at the URL https://apdt.com/trainer-search and the Certification Council for Professional Dog Trainers has a search option at: http://www.ccpdt.org/dog-owners/certified-dog-trainer-directory. The ADPT site includes services offered in their results as well as contact information and the trainer's website.

Make sure you research each trainer fully, looking for different certifications and evidence of continuing education in training dogs and understanding their behavior. Look to see if they mention specific work with rescued dogs and behavioral consultations, and make sure that you agree with their training philosophy and methods. You can also browse Yelp reviews and Google the trainer's name to look for positive or negative feedback from other clients.

I have had both adult rescued dogs and dogs that I raised from puppies from a professional hobby breeder. The love that I feel for each of them is different but equally strong.

When I lay quietly with my dogs who I have raised from puppies, I think about how I have loved them since they were tiny, that I helped raise them from little eight-week-old puppies to big strong dogs, and that I will love them all the way through their senior years. I have photos of them starting the day they were born and can look at their parents' photos to see who they look like. From the moment I signed the paperwork and put them in the car, I felt that they had had the best life a puppy could ever ask for and that it was my duty to ensure that their lives stayed that good. It is a maternal feeling, that they are like children to me for me to protect and nurture and care for their entire lives.

The love for my rescued dogs was equally strong, but I felt that we had rescued each other in a sense, and that it was my job to protect them from ever having another abusive or scary moment. With Babe I felt less of a dog mom to her and more of a best friend and faithful companion who was by my side through thick and thin. I would never know what had truly happened to our Basset Hound, Maggie, or my sweetheart foster, Destiny, before they came to us, but I felt an overwhelming sense that I would never let them feel fear and desperation ever again. I felt like I had been given the important duty of never letting anything bad happen to them ever again, that they were precious souls put into my trust.

No matter whether you brought your puppy home from puppy paradise with an amazing breeder, or rescued a puppy or grown dog from a bad situation, your love for them will be equally strong. And the best part: the love you get from them will be the same no matter what, as long as you treat them right and practice love, laugh and woof every day of your life.

As the years go by...

Whether you've started off your canine/human relationship during puppyhood or with a rescued adult dog, eventually the hard work that you put into training your dog through positive reinforcement, patience and repetition will pay off and you will achieve a beautiful friendship with your dog. This friendship, this bond, is like nothing else that you have with another being. It is unique because we are different species who come together to love and rely on each other. You are best friend, parent, caretaker and head of household all in one to your dog. This is the precious outcome that is worth all of the downsides of owning a dog that I outlined in Chapter 4, the reward for all of your dedication and hard work.

Some of my favorite moments in my life and with my dogs are so simple, like walking side by side off-leash through our back yard or going on long walks and hikes and just letting them sniff everything that they want for as long as they want, or holding onto their antlers for them when they chew them. We started this during puppyhood when I would give them their antlers to chew on instead of furniture or clothing, and both Jackson and Tinkerbell bring me their antlers to hold while they chew them. My heart melts when Jackson goes back to his pre-Tinkerbell days and brings me the torn up shark toy, Sharkie, to play tug-o-war because he specifically wants to play with me for a few minutes.

At some point you may ponder getting a second dog, which has pros and cons. When I had just Babe, she went everywhere with me except to work, but my life was perfectly suited for that during those years because I went to friends' homes often, to dinner at each of my parents' homes on weekends, and was single without children. It was easy to take one dog with me everywhere I wanted to go, I just tossed her travel bag of food, bowls, blanket and toys into my car and off we went.

The plus side of two dogs is that they have each other and often become a bonded pair like Jackson and Tinkerbell. I love to see them interact with each other in their special dog language that I do not always understand. I love watching them make eye contact in the yard, which heralds the start of a new game of Zoomies, which consists of them racing around the yard at top speed playfully chasing each other. I love to watch their daily games of Bitey-Face in which they snarl and growl and wrestle with their mouths open and their brilliant white teeth gnashing at each other without actually ever touching one another.

Of course with each dog comes an additional set of vet bills, additional food and medicine, and, of course, the need for extra patience. It means making sure that two dogs are cared for in case of an emergency or in the horrible scenario in which something happens to you.

Kids and Dogs

Kids and dogs can be the best of friends; my brothers and I grew up with our dogs playing an integral role in our family life, and all of my best memories of childhood include our Labrador retrievers. In order for this friendship to flourish and for both the children and the dogs to be happy and safe, it is as important to teach children how to act around a dog, as it is to teach a dog how to act around children.

I recently watched a viral video of a child in diapers who chased the family dog around the kitchen tormenting the dog while the parents watched, laughing and recording a video of the situation. The toddler smacked the dog on the face, hit it hard on the top of the head and the back, grabbed the dog and tried to climb on it, over and over again. The dog made continual eye contact with the child's mother and ran from the child every time it came near him with his tail tucked under him and his ears down, clearly afraid and unhappy. The mother did nothing to stop the abuse of the dog by the toddler, and abuse it most certainly was as the child repeatedly smacked the dog hard with an open hand.

My heart broke as I watched the video, knowing that the child would continue to treat the dog that way and that the dog would either suffer the abuse for its entire life or that the dog would finally break down and growl at or bite the child and end up in trouble and possibly put down or re-homed. The mother's response should have been to immediately correct her child, reprimand him by explaining to never pet or touch an animal that way, and show him the correct way to gently pet a dog.

Whether you bring your dog home as a puppy or a grown dog, it is critical that parents teach their children about how to be around the dog, including:

- ✓ How to pet the dog gently with soothing stroking motions.
- ✓ Areas to pet and areas to avoid: the sides, back, chest and under the chin are good spots; the top of the head and tail are not.
- ✓ It is never all right to grab the dog's fur, mouth, ears or tail with their hands.
- ✓ They should not hug the dog or try to press their face against the dog's face.
- ✓ They should not try to restrain the dog if it wants to walk away.
- ✓ They should not remove or insert toys, bones, food or treats from/into the dog's mouth
- ✓ It is not acceptable to lie on, climb on, or try to ride the dog.
- ✓ Hitting the dog is always off limits.

It is also important to watch children and their food, candy, and gum around the dog. One Christmas, one of our human children received some Hershey kisses while attending her school Christmas party. A generous child, she decided to wrap a few kisses in each of the Christmas gifts that she was giving to family members before putting the gifts under the tree. Later that day we went out for a few hours. Our dogs were older and had free run of the home. When we returned, one of the dogs had ripped open all of the gifts that our daughter had wrapped, leaving the others untouched. We were baffled until we asked, "Did you put some sort of food in your gifts?"

Fortunately, the dogs were all right, and the amount of chocolate that they consumed was not enough to be harmful. With kids in the house, dog owners must be extra diligent to ensure that candy, gum with or without Xylitol, soda, raisins and other food is not left in places that dogs can reach.

Toys can also be hazardous to dogs, particularly small plastic pieces, doll clothes and fast food toys. One of the most nerve-wracking items that our youngest girl loves the most is a small round lip balm that is approximately the size of a golf ball. These, along with small rubber bouncing balls and Ping-Pong balls, make me nervous because they pose a choking hazard.

Myth: Getting a Dog Will Teach A Child How To Be Responsible

I wish I could mince words on this, but I cannot. Getting a dog to teach a child to be responsible is one of the most irresponsible things that a parent can do. Getting a dog because the children want one, even if the adults do not, is equally absurd and unfair to the dog.

Adding a dog to the family should only happen when the adults are fully aware of the responsibilities, financial costs, time commitment and training required to raise a healthy, happy, well cared for dog. If the adults do not want a dog, they should not get one, no matter how much the children beg and plead. Raising a dog properly is something that requires maturity, a commitment of as long as twenty years, financial resources and someone who already knows how to be responsible.

Children can learn how to be responsible dog owners by learning from their parents, watching how they care for the dog, and participating in the dog's care under the parent's supervision. Turning over complete responsibility for important tasks like feeding or exercising the dog is simply unfair to the dog.

Kids are still learning how to manage their time and remembering to do chores and take care of their responsibilities. Many American kids are involved in extra-curricular activities and have substantial homework most weeknights along with their sports, birthday parties and other activities on weekends. Adding in the responsibility for remembering to feed the dog before and after school each day or to take it for a walk is risky; the dog will suffer if these important things are forgotten. When you add in monitoring the dog's health, performing maintenance like ear cleaning, grooming, monthly heartworm medicines, cleaning up after the dog, training the dog and other essential dog related tasks, the likelihood of the dog's level of care suffering is even greater.

A good way to teach children to be responsible for a dog is to give them specific guided instruction under adult supervision at the time the task needs to be done. Although all dog care is my responsibility, I will sometimes ask the kids to feed the dogs and I provide all of the details and then supervise to make sure that it is done correctly.

For example, instead of asking them in the morning to feed the dog, I will ask them at the time the feeding needs to happen, saying, "They each get one cup of food and three squirts of Red Krill oil. Make them sit and wait before you put the bowls down and then make them wait until you say 'ok'." This teaches them how to do the task without the worry that they will forget. They can learn day-to-day responsibility doing other things that do not involve living, breathing, feeling creatures, like taking out the garbage or vacuuming their rooms.

I love kids and I'm amazed at the maturity and intelligence that so many of them display. I am also a realist. When you think about the lifespan of a dog compared to the time that your kids live with you at home, it is likely that your kids will at first be too young to fully care for a dog, and then they'll reach the age when their school, activities and friends take up their time and attention, leaving the dog uncared for or in the care of the parents. It is better to only get the dog when the parents are fully on board and ready to take on the care, with or without the assistance of the children.

Mental exercise versus physical exercise

As magical as dog ownership is, every now and then you and your dog are not going to sync, and his boundless energy is not going to match your energy level. As much as I thrive on Jackson and Tinkerbell's high energy levels, sometimes things like a headache or cold strikes and I want nothing more for them to just lay and sleep with me. At two and four, they are great at this now, but I will never forget having the flu on a day when my husband had to go out of town on business during Jackson's puppyhood.

I had been at work that day and left around lunchtime to go home after it was obvious that I had a fever and had no business being in the office. As I drove home I knew that Jackson was going to be bouncing off the walls from being crated all morning. His dog sitter had already been to the house for his potty and play session, but I still doubted that he would be at all interested in spending the day laying around quietly with a flu ridden human.

I arrived home and let him out of his crate. We went outside so he could go potty and then headed back inside. I curled up in a ball on the sofa while he happily chewed on a dog toy. I was grateful beyond belief that he was being so calm. I was dreading him going into his crazy puppy mode that required me to follow him through the house watching his every move. Somehow, though, he knew that I was not right and instead of becoming my wild child puppy, he curled up next to me on the sofa and slept all afternoon with me. When my husband called to check in with me, I was in awe of Jackson, telling him, "He just seems to know I'm sick, he's been so calm and just laid next to me!"

I cannot recall the number of times I have fallen back on mental challenges to entertain the dogs when physical exercise is not an option. There is at least one week each winter when the temperatures in the Chicago suburbs go to well below zero and it is too cold for the dogs to do much more outside than relieve their bowels and bladders and race back inside.

Conversely, there are the weeks during the summer that are close to 100, which means that my dogs want nothing more than to sleep across the air conditioning vents. There was my knee surgery, my husband's broken ankle and a few other injuries where we could not take them for long walks or do much for them outdoors and we have made up games for them in addition to hide and seek, like finding hidden treats and playing with their educational dog toys that require they work on puzzles to find food.

Co-Sleeping with Dogs

Dogs are pack animals and want to be with their humans whether awake or at night. When you have two crates, as mentioned previously, it allows you to bring your dog into your bedroom as young puppies and sleep safely in their nighttime crate. After they can be trusted to not go to the bathroom in your bed or bedroom and you know they will not chew on things that might hurt them, they can graduate to a dog bed in your room or your human bed.

Jackson and Tinkerbell both have slept with us in our bedroom since their first night. The only nights that they have not is if they were sick and we anticipated frequent potty breaks, and during those nights either my husband or I slept on the sofa on our main floor so that we could get outside more quickly, usually with the sick dog on the sofa or on the floor next to whomever was on sick dog duty. In addition to wanting their company at night and knowing that they want ours, there are some practical and safety reasons that I want the dogs near me.

With the dogs in our room with us, I know that they can access me if they have to make an emergency outdoor visit in the middle of the night. Although their diet does not usually vary and I make sure they do all of their business on their last potty break of the night, things still happen and I know that they can wake me to let me know that they would like to go out.

Secondly, in the event of an emergency, I have them with me, whether it is a smoke detector, a tornado or storm warning or something else. I keep leashes and harnesses in the bedroom in case I must take them out of the room under my control to go to the basement or outside through the front door. That way I do not have to find them in other parts of the house; they are already with me. A harness can be important and life saving because a fearful dog may easily slip out of a regular collar, so I like to keep a harness that can even be used to pick them up if needed.

Pet Sitters and Boarding Kennels

Things happen and dog owners often must go places without warning, like work related travel, family emergencies, overnight events with kids and other reasons. In order to be prepared, you should always have a list of resources that can care for your dog as well as set of instructions for how to take care of your dog.

Make sure you have multiple options of caretakers for your dog in an emergency, including boarding kennels, dog sitting services or friends, family or neighbors who you can trust with a garage code or a key to your house. Keep this list on-hand somewhere easily accessible as well as on your phone or tablet so that you can access it on your own or send it to someone who is helping you in an emergency situation. Include their name, phone number, address and email information as well as their relationship to you. You can also print it on a business card size piece of paper or card stock and put it behind your driver's license clearly labeled "dog caretaker information, please contact in the event of emergency" particularly if you are the only adult in your household.

Although feeding the dog and taking the dog outside seem to be self-explanatory, having a set of instructions with everything your dog care provider needs to know will give you peace of mind. I keep a binder for Jackson and Tinkerbell and update it frequently. You can find a blank template for creating your own binder on my website at www.lovelaughwoof.com/tools.

My binder includes information on the type of food that they eat, what times they eat, how much, as well as a backup brand, flavor and where to purchase. I also have information on any medicine that they take, heartworm preventative brand, dosage and date, their training commands and the types of treats that they consume. There is a listing of medical issues that they have, contact information in case they cannot get in touch with me, and everything else that someone would require to step into my world and care for my home and my dogs for as long as needed.

In Case Your Dog Outlives You

As much as we do not want to think about this, it is critical to plan for your dog in case something happens to you so that her future is not chaotic and she does not land in a shelter or in a bad home. Earlier this year I volunteered to be the rescue transport for two beautiful senior Labradors, a bonded pair named Gypsy and Coco, whose owner had died suddenly and whose adult children could not take the dogs. They were rescued by a Labrador rescue and flown from southern Indiana to northern Illinois by a private pilot who does rescue transportation. I was their transportation from the airport to the veterinarian who would check them out before they went to the next stop, their foster home.

It was obvious that this bonded pair had been well loved and that they were terrified about everything that was happening to them. They remained glued to each other's side, their beautiful soulful Labrador eyes looking sad and scared, their dispositions sweet but clearly depressed.

Once at the vet, they wouldn't get out of my car, even backing themselves up into a corner where I could not get to pick them up and out of the car. It took almost an hour to get Gypsy positioned so that I could pick her up and physically remove her from the car. Coco was so panicked by not be touching her as I picked Gypsy up and set her down on the driveway that he nearly leapt out of the back of my SUV to make sure he was near her again. Fortunately

Gypsy and Coco quickly found a new forever home together and their ordeal is now over.

Excellent professional/hobby breeders will typically allow their puppy buyers to bring their dogs back to them at any point in the dog's life so that their dogs never find themselves in a shelter or a "free to a good home" advertisement. This is also useful and applicable if the owners pass away and is something that should be included in the owner's will or post-mortem instructions.

Many rescue organizations have this same rule in place for the same reason. Once they have helped a rescue dog find a home they do not want the dog to find its way back in a shelter facing uncertainty again; they would prefer to find a new home with another approved adopter. This is something to consider when choosing where you get a puppy or grown dog in case of an unforeseen tragedy. It is similar to having car insurance; you don't want to have to use it but it is there if you ever require it.

If you do not have a breeder or rescue group to take your dog in if you pass away, you will want to have the conversation with your family and friends and identity someone who has the proper residence, financial income and lifestyle to properly care for your dog for the rest of its life. Make sure you clearly make provisions for this in your own will and work with your lawyer and your financial planner to ensure that any funds that you leave for your dog's care are distributed correctly.

Preventing Lost Dogs

As an avid social media user, I see far too many postings of lost dogs. Social media is a great tool for helping spread the word and help locate lost dogs, but it breaks my heart each and every time as I think about how scared and confused they must be out in the world on their own. With training, planning and some common sense practices, you can minimize the risk of your dogs being separated from you.

Front Door

Think about all of the different people that come to your front door or other entrance to your home and the excitement that it gives to your dog to see who is there when you open it. From friends and family to the UPS delivery person, pizza guy, solicitors, Girl Scouts, and service providers, the average home has people coming and going frequently. Because of this, it is critical to train your dog to obey the Stay command at a designated place away from your door.

Stay is one of the commands in dog training that I've previously mentioned can mean life or death, and the entry to your home is one of those places where it is essential that your dog obey you. As you teach your dog to stay, remember to practice repeatedly near the entrance to your home, putting your dog in the Stay position several feet away and using that location each time. It is a good idea to first practice just touching the doorknob before advancing to opening the door. Eventually you can add people to your training sessions with someone coming through the door while your dog waits. Use your leash during those sessions until you are absolutely certain that your dog understands the command and what to do when you open the door.

In addition to training your dog, there are some habits that you can adopt each time you open the door to the outside world. After putting my dogs in the stay position, I always check to make sure that the screen door is closed before I fully open the front door. I have had well meaning people open the screen door for me, but I want the screen door closed as an extra barrier between my dogs and the outdoor world if I only want to have a conversation and I'm not actually letting anyone or anything through the door. I have actually scolded people who have opened our screen door and told them to never open someone's screen door because they don't know if they are about to let a dog or cat out of the house.

Body blocking the front door with your legs and lower body is also important in case your dog breaks her stay. I have noticed that I still do this, even through my dogs' stay is very reliable at this point in their lives. I have my feet spread apart but my knees somewhat together so that I can bend as needed to prevent a curious Labrador from sneaking past me on either side. This is particularly useful when you have to open the door wide to bring a pizza box inside your home, which is, in my opinion, one of the more nerve wracking scenarios for dog owners because the door is open very wide, the smell of food is strong in the air, and there isn't a person coming in or out to block the dog's path if they decide to run through the door.

If you have any uncertainty about whether or not your dog is ready to stay and not run out the open door, putting your dog in his or her kennel is a safe option, particularly if you have someone who will be coming in and out like a repair person or during a party. You can also continue to use the leash as you continue to work on their skills.

Another best practice is to keep your screen doors locked during nice weather when you have your doors open. We learned this while enjoying a lovely afternoon at a friend's house on a warm spring day. Our friends' dog noticed something outside and ran to the front door, jumping up and hitting the screen door handle just right. He opened the door on his own and ran out into the world. Fortunately his owner got him back quickly and he was not harmed, but from that day on we have locked our own screen door whenever we have our front door open.

Fenced Yard and Gates

A fenced in yard is a substantial convenience to dog owners and is a great place to play with and exercise your dog. However, a fenced in yard is not fool proof or 100% secure, and for that reason I strongly urge all dog owners to always accompany their dogs into the yards instead of sending the dog into the yard unattended.

Having lived without a fenced in yard for many years, I did what many dog owners do after moving into a home with a fenced yard and simply opened the door each time to let my senior dogs go out and explore and spend time outdoors. I went out with them often to play and have fun, but mostly I waited by the door for them to ask me to be let inside again. I trusted them that they would not do puppy behaviors like jumping the fence or eating contraband items.

One morning I was waiting for Dutch and Maggie to come inside. I could see Maggie wandering around sniffing the yard but could not see Dutch. Each time I called his name, Maggie turned her head to the gate on the side of the house where I could not see the fence. We did this several times before I thought that it seemed bizarre and went outside to investigate. As I rounded the house I panicked as I saw the gate wide open and no Dutch in sight. Still wearing my pajamas, I shut the gate behind me and sprinted into our front yard and looked down the street in both directions. There was my ten year old Dutch trotting along the sidewalk halfway down the block to the local park. "Dutch, WHOA!" I yelled, and he stopped and turned to look at me. "Dutch, SIT!" I commanded and he sat. I ran across the street to intercept him before he could cross on his own and walked him back to the house safe and sound.

Not knowing if he had jumped up and opened up the latch on the gate, or if one of our kids or one of the neighborhood kids had left it open the night before, I demanded we put locks on both gates. Of course the locks only worked until the meter reader from the electric company needed to read our meter, and we changed them out for mountain climbing carabineers, so that humans could manipulate them but dogs could not. Ever since that day, I have checked both gates each and every time the dogs have gone outside, no matter the weather or time of day. It only takes a few seconds and I have found an open gate on more than one occasion and diverted disaster by noticing it before the dogs did.

When Jackson came home I started the practice of staying outside with him the entire time he was outside, checking the gates and then remaining outside with him to make sure he did not slip under or go over the fence or slip through an open gate if one of the kids came through. This way I also make sure he does not eat anything harmful or do something that could hurt him, and it gives me an opportunity to play with him and interact with him. I can also monitor his bladder output and bowel movements to keep track of his health.

I go outside with both dogs in all weather, and I find myself the only human actually playing with my dogs outside, whether it is running through the snow with them or throwing their ball or flying disc. What started as a safety measure has also turned into a bonding experience with them, and it is something that I plan on doing every day of their lives. As a result, I have noticed that if I run into the house for a second that they tend to follow me to check in with me visually because I am their leader.

Moving to a New Home

Moving to a new home is a situation in which dogs can easily become lost. If you are moving locally, you can board your dog with a boarding kennel or pet sitter when you are moving from one place to another. Another option is to make sure that your dog's kennel is the last thing to be moved from your old home and the first thing to be moved into the new home. That way your dog can safely hang out in her crate while doors are opened and people and things are going in and out of the house. If you do not have a crate, you can confine your dog to one room or keep her on a leash. Find a family member or friend to hang out with your dog while she is confined or on her leash on moving day.

Make sure you check the fence in your new home to ensure that there are not places where your dog can go over or under, and to confirm that the gates are in working order. As mentioned earlier, check the gates to ensure that they are closed each time you go outside with your dog.

Take your dog on leashed walks around the neighborhood to let him smell and investigate the new area to increase his chances of finding his way home should he get lost or escape from the yard or house. I use the word "home" when the dogs and I arrive at our home after each walk just in case they are ever lost and someone tells them to go home. This is easy to do, and I have learned that my dogs can pick up on the names of different things by repeatedly using a simple word.

Parties and Social Gatherings

In the same way that moving increase the chances of your dog being lost because of people coming and going and doors opening frequently, parties and social gatherings are also a common reason that dogs become lost. Although your dog may love being part of a party and social gathering, the safest place for your dog is tucked away in her crate or with you on her leash, at least for large gatherings. Smaller parties are easier to manage as you can make sure that you know where your dog is as each guest arrives or leaves, and you can make her stay or hold onto her collar while the door is open. Open houses and large parties are problematic when people are continually coming and going, particularly if your guests are not dog savvy themselves.

If you have a crate in your bedroom as I suggest, you can put on music or the television, putting a few drops of lavender oil on a cotton ball or cloth near her crate, and settle your dog away from the frenzy of people so that he or she can relax in private. You can bring her out to mingle and visit on leash for awhile; the excitement and mental energy used will likely wear her out so much that she will happily sleep the rest of the party. After the guests have departed you can get her out, take her outside and then shower her with plenty of attention.

I have had plenty of guilt when we had large social events at our home with around fifty guests and I locked our people loving dogs away in our bedroom. I know they would have loved interacting with so many people and they would have been fawned over and showered with affection, but the risk of losing one of them through an open door, along with not being able to monitor what they were eating or even drinking, was sufficient to put my guilt to rest and do the safest thing and tuck them away in their kennels for their own safety. As the number of guests begins to dwindle, you can bring him out on leash to mingle and meet people.

If You Simply Do Have To Give Up Your Dog

I am not going to mince words here: the dog overpopulation problem is not just due to puppy mills and not spaying and neutering dogs. Those are immense problems and do contribute heavily, but the problem is also caused by people giving up on their dogs and dumping them in shelters or worse, out in the street or wilderness to fend for themselves.

If the problem were limited to over-breeding, we would not see grown dogs left alone and terrified in shelters or wandering as strays. We would not see senior dogs dropped off for just the crime of becoming elderly, or young energetic dogs abandoned for having too much energy, becoming too big or shedding too much. We would not see dogs tossed aside because new human babies were born. There is one reason for these dogs to be left without a human and a home: their owners were not committed to making their situation work, either because they did not realize an issue could be solved or simply because they did not care.

There are sometimes legitimate reasons for re-homing a dog, like not being able to find a place to live that allows the dog, or extremely dire financial situations. In these situations, a truly committed dog owner may have to search more for a pet friendly apartment or home outside of their desired area or price range or even take a second job. When faced with the choice of their owner being away an extra ten or twenty hours a week or being left alone and terrified at a kill shelter and ultimately put to death, your dog will choose the second job or the longer commute every single time.

When I rented and moved to a new state, I had very few options but I was still able to find an apartment that allowed my Labrador Retriever. In my younger years I have had some lean times where I had to live off of peanut butter and jelly sandwiches for a week because I could either pay an unexpected veterinary bill or purchase groceries. I chose to care for my dog; getting rid of her was never an option to me. I would have done anything legal to make sure that she was cared for and by my side.

If you absolutely must re-home your dog, the first option is to try to work with a rescue group assuming you do not have the option of returning the dog to the breeder. If you have a purebred dog and you purchased him from a reputable breeder you may have a first refusal clause in your contract and your dog can go back to your breeder to be re-homed. Otherwise a rescue group is definitely the best option.

Many rescue organizations are foster based, so your dog will go live in a home with a foster parent until the rescue group can find a suitable forever home. Rescue groups can only save as many dogs as they have fosters for, and there are never enough foster homes for all the dogs that need help. Expect to pay a fee or donation to help pay for your dog's veterinary care as rescue groups are funded entirely by donations and adoption fees. Rescue groups often have vet bills that far exceed the adoption fee because of the number of dogs who come in who have heart worms and other parasites and health issues.

If you cannot find a rescue group to take your dog, search for a no-kill shelter, or minimally low-kill shelter. Some shelters have more success placing dogs into homes than others. In some parts of the country, dogs only have about twenty-four hours to be pulled by a rescue group or adopted by someone before being euthanized. For many dogs, being surrendered to a shelter is virtually guaranteed to be a death sentence because the shelters are so full of abandoned dogs.

Although the "free to a good home" method of finding a new home for a dog is nothing new, there are an alarming number of dogs available on sites like Craigslist. It may seem like a great way to find a good home for your dog, but turning your dog over to strangers can have mixed results. Some people will provide loving, safe and permanent homes, but without the approval process done by rescue organizations and many shelters, your dog is going into a completely uncertain future. A better alternative is to try to place your dog with friends or friends of friends rather than with strangers from an Internet site. Also, you can reach out to your veterinarian or your dog trainer to see if they have contacts in rescue who can help you.

Getting rid of your dog should be the absolute last resort for all dog owners. There are professional trainers who can help with behavioral issues. If you are unable to financially provide for your dog, try setting up an online fundraising page to get you through troubled times until you can add an additional source of income. If you are in a situation where you cannot find a place to live, see if a friend or family member can temporarily care for your dog while you keep searching for a suitable home.

The Senior Years

Just like humans, dogs get old and their bodies start to fail them. Their bladders and bowels are less reliable and they get less notice from their body to their brain that they need to go outside. They become more likely to have accidents in the house, and they feel shame when they have an accident. Unlike puppies, senior dogs know that they should not eliminate their bodily waste in the home, but sometimes they simply cannot help it.

This is once again time for Love, Laugh, Woof to come into play. Love, understanding, and patience is so important so that you do not get mad at them or punish them for something that they could not help. Instead of getting angry, the senior years are a time to adjust your dog's potty schedule to include more frequent trips outside on a regular schedule so that they get more opportunities to go throughout the day. This could mean finding friends to help or hiring a dog sitter. We ended up keeping our dog sitter's daily potty visits even after Jackson was a grown dog because by that point Maggie was well into her senior years and we knew that a midday potty break would be a welcome relief for both of them, but particularly her aging bladder.

As your dog ages their muscles will start to weaken, joints will hurt them, and they will be less interested in playing, preferring instead to have a nice firm orthopedic bed to sleep. Your walks may grow shorter, but those walks are for their enjoyment first and foremost, so patience is important to give them as much time as they want to sniff the day's scents and go over their version of the day's trending stories.

Caring for a senior dog is one of the most special things you will do. Yes, it is heart- wrenching to watch your once energetic best friend slow down and play less and sleep more, but as their best friend and companion, it is the promise that you made to them when you brought them home. It is sometimes messy and terrible, but it is part of the job. Your vet bills will go up, and in some instances you will feel like you are running a doggie assisted living center; and you are. For a while when we had Babe, Dutch and Maggie we had an entire kitchen drawer full of senior dog medicines and supplements and a daily checklist to ensure that each dog had the correct treatment.

As a senior dog owner, I have cleaned up all of the following: giant puddles of urine, watery diarrhea in every room of our downstairs (on the same occasion), bloody vomit, you name it. My senior dogs are the reason I own multiple carpet cleaners and a cabinet full of carpet cleaning options. I have paid for barium tests, x-rays of every kind, dental extractions, dental cleanings, pain medicines, human blood pressure medicines, and prescription diets. I have fed sick dogs by hand, cooked special meals for them, picked them up from falling down in their own excrement and bathed them and washed the kitchen floor upon coming home from work.

I have cried hot, ugly tears of sadness, desperation and frustration at watching my senior dogs decline, and I have agonized over whether or not it was "time" for their final vet visit. And finally, I have laid on the floor with them at the vet's office, always on the particular dog's special blanket, and held back my own tears and grief so as not to stress them, and held them and stroked their faces while the veterinarian gave them the final two shots to send them to the rainbow bridge. With each dog, I have held back my own heart break until I knew they had passed away before breaking down, because I knew that they would not want to see my cry any more than they had ever wanted to see me cry.

I have done all of these things through their senior years and into the final moments of their lives because every dog owner should commit to doing these things the moment they bring a canine life into their home. There was no question as to whether or not it will be too hard or too sad; it is what I owed them, what they deserved from me, and I would never have given them any less because I loved them as much as I love every family member.

I have heard of dog owners who would not be in the same room as their dogs during euthanasia because it was too hard for them, and I find that cruel and cowardly. Of course it is hard, of course it is sad, and of course it is heart breaking. But our job as dog owners is to be strong for our dogs, to be by their side, to keep them from being afraid and alone. We are their caretakers for all of their lives and the only place for an owner at the end of a dog's life, should be by his or her side. They have loyally stood by ours with their trusting nature and unwavering dedication and love, to have and to hold, for better or for worse, in good times and in bad, until death parts us.

BIBLIOGRAPHY

The Labrador Retriever Club. "The Labrador Retriever Illustrated Standard." *The Labrador Club. Com.* The Labrador Retriever Club, Inc. 2002. Web.

"Dog Breed Selector - What Kind Of Dog Should I Get?" - *American Kennel Club.* American Kennel Club, n.d. Web. 31 Mar. 2016. <http://www.akc.org/find-a-match>.

"Animal Planet." *Animal Planet.* Animal Planet, n.d. Web. 31 Feb. 2016. <http://www.animalplanet.com/breed-selector/dog-breeds.html>.

"Labrador Retriever Breed Standard." *The Labrador Club.* The Labrador Retriever Club, 31 Mar. 1994. Web. 31 Mar. 2016. <http://www.thelabradorclub.com/subpages/show_contents. php?page=Breed+Standard>.

"The Association of Professional Dog Trainers." *Dog Trainer Search.* Association of Professional Dog Trainers, n.d. Web. 31 Mar. 2016. <https://apdt.com/trainer-search>.

"Certified Dog Trainer Directory - CCPDT." *CCPDT.* Certification Council for Professional Dog Trainers, n.d.

Web. 31 Mar. 2016. <http://www.ccpdt.org/dog-owners/certified-dog-trainer-directory./>.

Boccone, Bud. "America's Best Friend: The Labrador Retriever." *AKC*. The American Kennel Club, 19 July 2015. Web. 31 Mar. 2016. <http://www.akc.org/learn/akc-gazette/americas-best-friend-the-labrador-retriever/>.

McVay, Julie. Shadowland Kennels, Obedience and Boarding. Personal communication and Puppy Packet, 2011.

About the Author

Lynn Stacy-Smith is a lifelong dog lover and author of the blog Love, Laugh, Woof. She is passionate about helping dog owners understand how to be compassionate dog owners as well as teaching humans about how to create a healthy and happy lifestyle for their pets. She lives in the far western suburbs of Chicago with her husband, three teenage stepchildren and Labrador Retrievers Jackson and Tinkerbell.

Printed in the United States
By Bookmasters